CITYSPOTS
SAN F

WHAT'S IN YOUR GUIDEBOOK?

Independent authors Impartial up-to-date information from our travel experts who meticulously source local knowledge.

Experience Thomas Cook's 165 years in the travel industry and guidebook publishing enriches every word with expertise you can trust.

Travel know-how Thomas Cook has thousands of staff working around the globe, all living and breathing travel.

Editors Travel-publishing professionals, pulling everything together to craft a perfect blend of words, pictures, maps and design.

You, the traveller We deliver a practical, no-nonsense approach to information, geared to how you really use it.

ABOUT THE AUTHOR

Kevin Massy is a journalist and author who swapped the London drizzle for the San Francisco fog and has never found his way back. His writing has appeared in *The Economist, The Independent, The Guardian* and *The San Francisco Chronicle*. This is his first foray into travel writing, which is testament indeed to San Francisco's inspirational qualities.

CITYSPOTS
SAN FRANCISCO

Kevin Massy

Thomas Cook

Written by Kevin Massy

Published by Thomas Cook Publishing
A division of Thomas Cook Tour Operations Limited
Company registration No: 3772199 England
The Thomas Cook Business Park, 9 Coningsby Road
Peterborough PE3 8SB, United Kingdom
Email: books@thomascook.com, Tel: +44 (0)1733 416477
www.thomascookpublishing.com

Produced by The Content Works Ltd
Aston Court, Kingsmead Business Park, Frederick Place
High Wycombe, Bucks HP11 1LA
www.thecontentworks.com

Series design based on an original concept by Studio 183 Limited

ISBN: 978-1-84848-163-3

First edition © 2009 Thomas Cook Publishing
Text © Thomas Cook Publishing
Maps © Thomas Cook Publishing/PCGraphics (UK) Limited
Transport map © Communicarta Limited

Series Editor: Lucy Armstrong
Production/DTP: Steven Collins

Printed and bound in Spain by GraphyCems

Cover photography (San Francisco's iconic cable cars ferry passengers around
the city) © Thomas Cook

CONTENTS

INTRODUCING
SAN FRANCISCO

Introduction 8
When to go 10
Bay to Breakers........................14
History 16
Lifestyle 18
Culture 20

MAKING THE MOST OF
SAN FRANCISCO

Shopping 24
Eating & drinking 26
Entertainment
 & nightlife 30
Sport & relaxation 32
Accommodation 34
The best of San Francisco ...38
Suggested itineraries 40
Something for nothing 42
When it rains 44
On arrival 46

THE CITY OF
SAN FRANCISCO

Downtown 58
The Central Districts 78
The West 92

OUT OF TOWN TRIPS

Angel Island & Sausalito ...106
North of the Bridge to
 the Valley & the Beach.....118

PRACTICAL INFORMATION

Directory 128
Emergencies 138

INDEX 140

MAPS

San Francisco 48
San Francisco
 transport map.....................52
Downtown 60
The Central Districts............80
The West 94
Around San Francisco.........108

SYMBOLS KEY

The following symbols are used throughout this book:

ⓐ address ☏ telephone ⓦ website address ⓔ email
🕓 opening times Ⓝ public transport connections ❶ important

The following symbols are used on the maps:

𝑖	information office	▦	points of interest
✈	airport	O	city
➕	hospital	o	large town
🛡	police station	=	motorway
🚍	bus station	—	main road
🚆	railway station	—	minor road
Ⓜ	metro/BART	—	railway
✝	cathedral	❶	numbers denote featured cafés & restaurants

Hotels and restaurants are graded by approximate price as follows:
£ budget price **££** mid-range price **£££** expensive

▶ *Alamo Square's 'Painted Ladies' exemplify the city's Victorian architecture*

Introduction

What is it about San Francisco that so captures the imagination? Even before the heady days of the Gold Rush catapulted this foggy peninsula to prominence in the 19th century, the City by the Bay held a magnetism for those in search of adventure and new opportunity. And while the elegant Victorian houses and historic cable cars suggest a city in love with its past, San Francisco's appeal continues to lie in its willingness to adapt to the times, to foster new ideas and to evolve. Today, the city celebrates culture and counterculture in equal measure. Gourmet restaurants, high-end retail and world-class museums rub shoulders with Buddhist temples, independent art galleries, juice bars, dive bars and gay bars. From the packed pavements of Chinatown to the margaritas and mariachi bands of the Mission, the flagship stores of Haight Street to the queens of the Castro, modern San Francisco

is a kaleidoscope of influences. Along with its diversity, the city prides itself on being at the forefront of change and sustainable 21st-century living. Visitors to San Francisco find themselves in a true world city, a centre of global finance that prefers corner stores to chain stores, a foodies' paradise that creates international cuisine with locally-sourced ingredients. As the epicentre of the beat and hippie movements, the city confirmed its status as a cradle of social activism, and its abundance of festivals, street fairs and parades enable modern-day San Franciscans to continue the tradition of personal expression. As a backdrop to its myriad urban charms, the city is blessed with breathtaking natural scenery, and Golden Gate Park and the Presidio provide bucolic escapes from the Bayside bars and bistros. Welcome to San Francisco, a city where global meets local, where hearts are famously left behind, and where freedom sips cappuccino in a sidewalk café.

San Francisco – the kind of place you might leave your heart

When to go

SEASONS & CLIMATE

With water on three sides and a famously hilly landscape, San Francisco has a unique climate. Even within the city, the topography of the land creates a series of microclimates that can lead to stark differences between the temperatures in the central districts and the coastal areas.

San Francisco does not experience the same warm summers as many other Californian cities. While a temperate year-round climate means that there is never a really bad time to visit, the most comfortable seasons are late spring (April to mid-May) and autumn (September to November). Winters see a moderate drop in temperature, with lows around 7–10°C (45–50°F), and rain is most likely in January and February. Due to the fog rolling in from the Pacific Ocean in summer, warm afternoons can quickly turn into chilly evenings.

ANNUAL EVENTS

February

Chinese New Year Festival Parade Forming nearly a third of San Francisco's population, the city's Chinese community comes out in force for an event that culminates with a giant parade complete with floats, fireworks and an enormous dragon. ⓦ www.chineseparade.com

May

Bay to Breakers An annual party that lights up the peninsula (see page 14). ⓦ www.ingbaytobreakers.com

Maker Faire Held in San Mateo on the last weekend of the month, this two-day tribute to geekdom and tech DIY brings the best of the Bay Area's inventors together for a celebration of gadgets, games and great ideas. And geekdom. ⓦ www.makerfaire.com

June
San Francisco Gay Pride This world-famous two-day event involves celebrations and performances in the Civic Center and the parade itself, which runs down Market Street on the Sunday. ⓦ www.sfpride.org

June–September
Stern Grove Festival Set in the beautiful surroundings of Stern Grove, this annual series of free concerts is one of the hidden gems of the summer months in San Francisco. ⓦ www.sterngrove.org

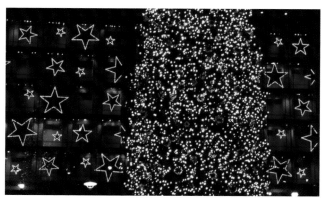

⬥ Holiday lights at Union Square

July

Fillmore Street Jazz Festival Paying homage to the icons that made the Fillmore district a jazz mecca in the post-war years, the annual extravaganza sees this diverse neighbourhood resound to the strains of live music and the smell of barbecues. ⓦ www.fillmorejazzfestival.com

August

Japantown Street Fair Japantown (or Nihonmachi) comes to life with free outdoor concerts including Taiko drum performances, Samurai exhibitions and rows of food stalls. ⓦ www.nihonmachistreetfair.org

September

San Francisco Blues Festival As the summer fog recedes, the city boogies to the blues at this popular two-day music event in the Marina. ⓦ www.sfblues.com

Folsom Street Fair This leather-and-latex fetish jamboree is a true one-of-a-kind spectacle involving 400,000 participants and attendees, with plenty of performances, exhibitors and exhibitionists. ⓦ folsomstreetfair.org

October

Oktoberfest by the Bay Drawing many of San Francisco's large German population – and other beer lovers – this annual knees-up sees a vast warehouse transformed into a giant Munich beer hall. ⓦ www.oktoberfestbythebay.com

Fleet Week An annual exhibition of air and naval hardware, culminating in a display by the US Navy's Blue Angels. The

views of this event from Telegraph Hill are worth the climb.
Ⓦ www.military.com/fleetweek

November & December
San Francisco does much to make Yuletide gay. The **Great Dickens Christmas Fair** (Ⓦ www.dickensfair.com) at the Cow Palace Exhibition Hall runs throughout December and does a good job of recreating Scrooge's London, complete with ale houses, merchants and entertainment. Tree-lighting ceremonies in Union Square and Ghirardelli Square take place in the week after Thanksgiving, kicking off the Holiday Season in earnest.

PUBLIC HOLIDAYS
New Year's Day 1 Jan
Birthday of Martin Luther King, Jr. 18 Jan 2010, 17 Jan 2011, 16 Jan 2012
Washington's Birthday/Presidents' Day 15 Feb 2010, 21 Feb 2011, 20 Feb 2012
Memorial Day 31 May 2010, 30 May 2011, 28 May 2012
Independence Day 4 July
Labor Day 7 Sept 2009, 6 Sept 2010, 5 Sept 2011, 3 Sept 2012
Columbus Day 12 Oct 2009, 11 Oct 2010, 10 Oct 2011, 8 Oct 2012
Veterans' Day 11 Nov
Thanksgiving Day 26 Nov 2009, 25 Nov 2010, 24 Nov 2011, 22 Nov 2012
Christmas Day 25 Dec

Bay to Breakers

If any one event sums up San Francisco's trademark eclectic and outrageous personality, it is Bay to Breakers, an annual foot race that runs, walks, whoops, dances and staggers its way across the city every third Sunday in May. Starting at the eastern edge of Downtown San Francisco (the Bay) and running to Ocean Beach (the Breakers), the event is the nearest thing the city has to Mardi Gras, closing down much of the town with its tens of thousands of participants.

The day starts with a handful of elite athletes who race across the 12 km (7 ½ mile) course in less time than it takes for the Powell cable car to get to Fisherman's Wharf. But the real event starts after the serious runners have cleared the field, and legions of San Franciscans and out-of-town visitors follow in their wake across the peninsula. Dressed in homemade costumes that run the spectrum from flamboyant to funny to downright freaky (and with many opting for no costume at all), participants push floats, mobile speakers and a host of other accessories along the course. Thousands of spectators turn out to cheer them on, with many residents along the route opening up their houses as refuelling stations and providing a roadside sound-track to the mobile orgy. Among the more determined participants, a group of runners dressed in salmon outfits traditionally runs the race 'upstream', starting at the finish and struggling head-on through the throng, with predictably chaotic consequences. Following the completion of the course, those who are still able to stand make their way from the beach to the Polo Fields in Golden Gate Park where the party continues with live music, food and general revelry. Participants are required to register to enter the official start and finish areas, but those who wish to get involved along the route only need to bring an open mind and a camera. For more information visit ⓦ www.ingbaytobreakers.com

◑ *It seems like the whole city turns out for the Bay to Breakers race*

History

When Sir Francis Drake sailed right past what is now San Francisco Bay in 1579, he gave the native Ohlone people living there a nearly 200-year reprieve from contact with European explorers. It was not until 1769 that a party of Spanish travellers arrived from Southern California, promptly claiming the land for the Spanish Crown and establishing a military outpost, named the Presidio of San Francisco. In 1776, the Catholic Church established the Mision San Francisco de Asis, today the city's oldest surviving building. Following the Mexican War of Independence, the area became part of Mexico in 1821, but remained so only until 1846 when California – and the nascent town of Yerba Buena on the northeast of the peninsula – was claimed for the United States. The sleepy town, renamed simply San Francisco, was about to undergo a massive population influx. Following the discovery of gold in Northern California in 1848, hundreds of thousands of fortune hunters flocked to the city, which quickly grew to accommodate its new residents and their new-found wealth. A swathe of bars, brothels, gambling parlours and opium dens formed the infamous Barbary Coast around the area that now covers Chinatown, North Beach and the Financial District. Flush with money, San Francisco's residents set about making their town respectable, building up a commercial city centre complete with hi-tech cable cars for public transportation and residential districts of wooden Victorian houses. The city's rise as a cultural and financial centre was so rapid that by the end of the 19th century it was known as 'the Paris of the West'. These heady days were not to last long.

On 18 April 1906, San Francisco experienced one of the most devastating earthquakes of modern times. The resulting fire destroyed nearly all of the structures to the east of Van Ness Avenue, reducing most of the city to ashes. A monumental rebuilding effort produced the blueprint for the present-day Downtown area. During the 20th century, the city continued to expand. In the 1950s and 1960s it became a refuge for a generation of disaffected youth who founded the beat and hippie movements, both characterised by a rejection of established authority. Throughout the 1970s the city continued its evolution as a centre of progressive thought as, when the love that had formerly dared not speak its name suddenly decided to shout it from the roof-tops, it became the launching pad of the global gay rights movement, producing such local, then national (and ultimately international) figures as Harvey Milk.

At the end of the 20th century, San Francisco again rose to international prominence as the centre of the dotcom internet revolution, with many companies in the city benefiting from the vast amount of money invested in the technology sector before its crash in 2000.

With its old-money families, Victorian houses, creaking cable cars, Haight Street hustlers, gay bars and dotcom billionaires, modern San Francisco is a testament to its own relatively brief, but wildly eventful, past.

Lifestyle

San Franciscans like to tell you that there's a world of difference between northern and southern California – and it's true. In contrast to the sun, sand and shallow celebrity down the coast in Hollywood, San Francisco sees itself as a more substantial, grown-up community, a place where high ideals trump high heels and where your carbon footprint is more important than your zip code. With one of the most affluent and educated populations in the United States, the compact city offers plenty of premium retail and fine dining opportunities, although fashion is less important than in Los Angeles and New York, and restaurants place more emphasis on wholesome, locally sourced dishes than on haute cuisine. The city's abundant nightlife is equally organic, with bars more likely to serve microbrews than Miller Lite and local bands and DJs playing small, intimate venues rather than arenas.

Environmental awareness is high on the lifestyle agenda: the city has the highest recycling rate of any in the United States and was the first in the country to ban plastic shopping bags. As the epicentre of the dotcom boom, San Francisco boasts a disproportionately large tech-savvy population, a fact underlined by the legions of locals who spend their days in neighbourhood coffee shops, glued to their (Apple) laptop computers. Above all, the city prides itself on its diversity and tolerance of alternative lifestyles. The presence of a large number of Latino and Chinese residents is underlined by the trilingual notices in many public areas, and a request for directions in English will often be answered by a quizzical look of non-comprehension.

As the first city in the United States to perform same-sex marriages (though these have now been banned), San Francisco confirmed itself as one of the most gay-friendly places in the country – to the delight of many residents but to the chagrin of those who decry the influence of liberal 'San Francisco values'; not that such categorisations bother San Franciscans, who see themselves – with some justification – as being at the forefront of change in 21st-century America.

◔ *Chinatown is just one suburb that reflects the city's multiculturalism*

Culture

San Franciscans are a remarkably cultured bunch. In this city, to characterise somebody as having a creative bent or being artistic by inclination is to bestow upon them a great compliment. Indeed, ever since it established its reputation as 'the Paris of the West', San Francisco has played host to a thriving cultural scene that these days leaves that of the real Paris distinctly in the shade. With less than a million inhabitants, the city today punches far above its weight in terms of cultural assets. Its dozens of museums feature exhibits ranging from fine- and modern art to African history to mechanical arcade games. The M.H. de Young Museum (see page 97) in Golden Gate Park is particularly worth visiting, as much for its architecture as for its vast collection of American art. Home to the country's largest private art and design university, San Francisco is brimming with young artists keen to show off their work, and while the cluster of theatres in proximity of Union Square has given rise to the 'Theater District' moniker, the area is at least as notable for its numerous boutique art galleries. On many weekends, Union Square itself turns into an impromptu art gallery for local artists. Theatre buffs also have plenty to choose from, including performances of internationally acclaimed productions at the American Conservatory Theater (see page 67) and the annual **San Francisco Shakespeare Festival** (ⓦ www.sfshakes.org), which includes free outdoor performances throughout the summer. The city also enjoys a thriving independent theatre scene at its many smaller playhouses, listings for which can be found in the free *SF Weekly* newspaper.

⬤ *Palm row at the M.H. de Young Museum*

It comes as absolutely no surprise that independent cinema flourishes in the local hot-house, art-house environment, with the **San Francisco International Film Festival** (Ⓦ www.sffs.org) and **San Francisco International LGBT Film Festival** (Ⓦ www.frameline.org/festival) bringing a fresh crop of productions to the city's screens each year. This is the kind of city where 90 minutes staring at an unintelligible succession of meaningless images will have cinema audiences emerging into the daylight dabbing at tears of genuine emotion rather than those of hollow, philistine derision. Classical music lovers are well catered for too: from September to June, the **Davies Symphony Hall** (Ⓐ 201 Van Ness Ave Ⓣ (415) 864-6000) plays host to a season of world-class performances, while, across the road, the War Memorial Opera House is home to both the San Francisco Opera and the San Francisco Ballet (see page 68). One of the lesser-known highlights of the city's musical calendar is the Stern Grove Festival (see page 11), a series of free outdoor performances that take place each summer amid stunning natural surroundings.

Much of the culture of San Francisco is accessible simply by walking the streets and taking in the city's eclectic buildings and historic monuments. To get a real insight into the city's architecture, consider signing up for one of the free San Francisco Walking Tours (see page 136) conducted by enthusiastic local volunteers who are happy to give you the benefit of their knowledge on everything from the bordellos of the Barbary Coast to the design of the Golden Gate Bridge.

▶ *A quintessential street of San Francisco*

MAKING THE MOST OF
San Francisco

Shopping

With its compact, pedestrian-friendly Downtown area, San Francisco is an ideal hunting ground for shoppers. The expanded Westfield San Francisco Center mall on Market Street (see page 69) contains a couple of colossal department stores as well as outlets for nearly every major American clothing and cosmetic chain. The high street retail district centres on Union Square, the site of two more department stores as well as a number of premium jewellery, homeware and clothing stores. For high rollers and fashionistas, the area directly to the east of Union Square, centred on Post Street, features exclusive boutiques as well as flagship stores for high-end couture brands. For designer labels without the designer price tags, the area around Union Square also offers a number of discount fashion retailers, including **Loehmanns** (ⓐ 222 Sutter St ❶ (415) 982-3215 Ⓦ www.loehmanns.com) and **Marshalls** (ⓐ 901 Market St ❶ (415) 974-5368 Ⓦ www.marshallsonline.com). Those seeking a break from multinational brands can take refuge in Maiden Lane, a pedestrianised street running east from the centre of Union Square and featuring independent clothes designers, jewellery boutiques and art galleries. Moving east into the financial district, the glass-ceilinged Crocker Galleria (see page 69) offers three levels of delights. Foodies should not miss the Ferry Building (see page 64), a temple to local cuisine and a perfect place to pick up a gourmet gift. For seasonal delights, the **farmers' market** (❶ (415) 291-3276) on Tuesday between 10.00 and 14.00 and Saturday between 08.00 and 14.00 is particularly worth visiting.

Away from Downtown, the city offers a number of self-contained retail districts specialising in local boutiques, craft stores and gift shops. Union Street in the Marina district has dozens of health and beauty stores mixed in with jewellers, home-furnishing shops and boutiques offering fashionably expensive clothing and accessories. The Upper Fillmore retail district features a similar mix of upmarket clothes stores and pampering parlours. For a truly unique retail experience, check out Castro Street between Market and 19th Streets, which offers trendy clothing boutiques and shoe shops alongside leather-goods stores, bookshops and stores catering to the male gay community. And if your trip is not complete without a San Francisco snow globe, the shops of Fisherman's Wharf will accommodate your every need – at special tourist prices.

⬥ Psychedelic-fantastic at Haight Ashbury

Eating & drinking

While nearly every kind of cuisine is represented among the city's hundreds of eateries, San Francisco specialises in Californian dishes that are big on fresh, local and seasonal ingredients.

San Franciscans pride themselves on being discerning diners, and restaurants cater to foodies of every stripe. The majority of the fine-dining establishments are clustered around the Financial District between Union Square and the Bay, although the south of Market (SOMA) and Pacific Heights areas also attract those wanting to drop a couple of hundred dollars a head. For the rest of us, there are plenty of reasonably priced restaurants all over the city.

Despite the attention to culinary detail, there is a lack of formality at most of the city's restaurants. Tipping is all but mandatory, with 15 per cent of the pre-tax total regarded as a baseline tip and 20 per cent or more appropriate for good service. Seafood is a big part of the local food scene, and the city's numerous sushi bars and fish restaurants offer the pick of the Pacific catch. For those in search of an authentic San Francisco experience, the 160-year-old wood-panelled Tadich Grill (see page 74) on California Street offers a slice of Gold-

PRICE CATEGORIES

The following categories reflect the cost of a two-course meal per person (excluding drinks and tip).

£ up to $10   ££ $10–20   £££ over $20

🔺 *Grilled branzino at the Tadich Grill*

Rush-era history, while the sequestered row of Mediterranean-inspired restaurants on Belden Lane has a range of seafood dining options with the rare opportunity for terrace dining.

The city's patchwork of ethnically distinct neighbourhoods provides a wealth of tasty options. As the supposed birthplace of the burrito, San Francisco has a formidable reputation for Mexican food, the best of which is to be found in the inexpensive *taquerias* (informal Mexican joints) of the Mission district. These restaurants offer far more than tacos: specialities include fajitas, enchiladas, quesadillas, burritos and, of course, margaritas. With large Chinese and Japanese populations, the city benefits from a variety of Asian cuisines, and the busy dim sum parlours of Chinatown provide a stark contrast to the sleepy noodle bars of Japantown. For those in the mood for Italian, North Beach offers everything from California-style pizzas to large plates of homemade pasta served family style. Other highlights include a wealth of inexpensive Thai and Vietnamese restaurants dotted throughout the Tenderloin district and a selection of bargain Indian eateries, many with a bring-your-own-beer policy.

Drinking is almost as important as eating in San Francisco, and the city boasts countless bars and pubs, many with happy

🔺 *The Mission's* taquerias *provide a wealth of cheap eats*

ON A MISSION: KNOW YOUR MEXICAN FOOD

burrito (bu-*ree*-to) A wheat tortilla containing beans, rice, meat or fish, guacamole, sour cream, salsa and lettuce

enchilada (enchi-*la*-da) Like a burrito, although usually made with corn tortillas, and covered with a chilli pepper sauce and sour cream

fajita (fa-*hee*-ta) Grilled vegetables and meat folded into a plain tortilla with salad, guacamole, salsa and cheese

quesadilla (kaysa-*dee*-ya) Toasted tortilla filled with cheese and sometimes other ingredients including meat, often served with salad, salsa and sour cream

taco A folded corn tortilla filled with fish or shredded meat, cheese, lettuce and salsa

tortilla A disc of unleavened bread made from either cornmeal or wheat

hours on week nights. Situated only a couple of hours from the vineyards of the Napa and Sonoma valleys, San Francisco is a wine-lover's paradise, and whether it's a $6 glass of merlot or a flight of wine pairings at one of the city's top restaurants, visitors have a wide selection of California vintages to choose from. Real-ale lovers are also in luck as the city boasts a number of local microbreweries. For those who want to stock up on picnic fodder, cater themselves or snag some gourmet gifts, the city offers plenty of full-service grocery stores, and the restored Ferry Building (see page 64) showcases much of what gives San Francisco a special place in the culinary world.

Entertainment & nightlife

The secret to a good night out in San Francisco is knowing not to start at Union Square. Somewhat counter intuitively, the city's main hotel and shopping district is perhaps its most barren in terms of nightlife, and those searching for bars and pubs in the vicinity will be disappointed to find only overpriced tourist traps and seedy sports bars. Even the Financial District, so well stocked with decent restaurants, has limited attraction for those looking for nightlife: aside from a few pricey bars that fill up with a bunch of bankers on weekday evenings, the area holds little for those looking to burn the midnight oil or dance the night away. For a livelier Downtown scene, visitors need to turn their sights south of Market, where clusters of pubs and trendy bars cater to the denim-clad designers and dotcommers who work on 2nd Street.

As any local will tell you, however, most of San Francisco's best nightlife is not found in Downtown at all. Instead, the main action takes place in the various neighbourhoods to the west and north, each delivering its own distinct experience. Directly north of the Financial District, North Beach provides a self-contained night on the town. In addition to its wealth of Italian restaurants, the area centered on Columbus Avenue offers a vast selection of bars, pubs and low-key live-music venues (it also features a row of less low-key strip joints). Moving west, the chic Marina district is the stomping ground of the city's bright, young, well-heeled things, and the bistros and cocktail bars of Union Street offer visitors a little slice of Santa Barbara by the bay.

In contrast, the Mission district, with its countless dive bars, *taquerias* and intimate live-music lounges, is pure San Francisco.

The area around Valencia and 16th Streets is tailor-made for pub crawls, with the all-night Mexican restaurants providing pit stops between bars. The neighbouring Castro district offers a number of decent restaurants, bars and dance clubs, the latter catering mainly to the gay community. The area around Haight Street provides a mixture of grungy Goth bars, Irish pubs, cheap eateries and small dance clubs featuring live DJs. Other noteworthy areas include Clement Street (for pubs and live music); Hayes Valley (for wine bars and creative dining); and the lively Polk Street corridor running north of Tenderloin (for good old-fashioned drinking holes). Due to the compact nature of the city, many of these main nightlife districts are only a short walk or a $5 to $10 cab ride from each other. With a few exceptions, most bars and pubs stay open until 02.00, with bartenders promptly collecting glasses – whether empty or not – around 20 minutes before closing time. Tipping is expected, with the rule of thumb being a dollar per drink.

San Francisco's vibrant live music scene is characterised more by small, intimate venues than packed arenas. Many local bands can be found playing at hole-in-the-wall venues such as Elbo Room (see page 89) and **Cafe du Nord** (ⓐ 2170 Market St ⓣ (415) 861-5016 ⓦ www.cafedunord.com), and even the city's flagship concert venues, **The Fillmore** (ⓐ 1805 Geary Blvd ⓣ (415) 346-4000 ⓦ www.thefillmore.com) and The Warfield (see page 76), have relatively modest capacities of 1,250 and 2,100 respectively. Movie theatres showing everything from Hollywood blockbusters to independent films are dotted throughout the city. For a comprehensive guide of what's playing, pick up a free copy of the *SF Weekly* newspaper or visit the *San Francisco Chronicle* site at ⓦ www.sfgate.com.

Sport & relaxation

SPECTATOR SPORTS
American football
Situated about 11 km (7 miles) south of Downtown, Candlestick Park plays host to San Francisco 49ers' home games throughout the season, which runs from the beginning of September to the end of December. A limited number of tickets are available for home games. ⓐ 490 Jamestown Ave ⓣ Tickets: (415) 464-9377 ⓦ www.sf49ers.com ⓝ Muni bus: 77X from Van Ness Ave, 78X from Richmond and Sunset districts, 79X from Financial District

Baseball
Opened in 2000, the AT&T Park is a great place to take in a ballgame, a hotdog and some stunning views of the Bay. During the season (April to September), single-game tickets are usually available. ⓐ 4 Willie Mays Plaza ⓣ Tickets: (415) 972-2000 ⓦ www.sfgiants.com ⓛ Ticket office: 08.30–17.30 Mon–Fri and during all home games ⓝ Muni metro: N and T lines to Second and King station

PARTICIPATION SPORTS
While most gyms in the city are members-only, the **Embarcadero YMCA** (ⓐ 169 Steuart St ⓣ (415) 957-9622 ⓦ www.ymcasf.org) offers visitors state-of-the-art facilities including a pool and racket-ball courts; day passes are $15 and a valid photo ID is required. Cyclists should not miss the chance to bike across the Golden Gate Bridge or on one of the many trails through Golden Gate Park; for bike hire and route suggestions, visit **Blazing Saddles**

(📞 (415) 202-8888 🌐 www.blazingsaddles.com), which has five locations throughout the city.

RELAXATION
Located a short bus ride west of Downtown, **Kabuki Springs and Spa** (📍 1750 Geary Blvd 📞 (415) 922-6000 🌐 www.kabukisprings.com 🕐 10.00–22.00) offers reasonably priced Japanese-style communal bathing and more expensive spa and massage services. The countless spas, nail salons and massage spots of the Union Street and Upper Fillmore retail districts also offer plenty of high-end pampering opportunities.

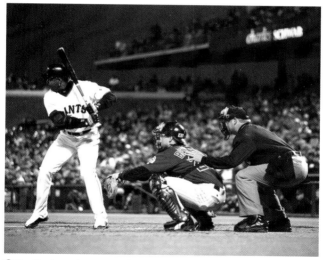

🔺 *The Giants are San Francisco's local baseball team*

Accommodation

San Francisco is not a cheap place to stay, even for the budget traveller. While many of the city's luxury hotels are worth visiting as tourist attractions in their own right, they charge eye-popping prices for a room. For more mortal budgets, there are bargains to be had in the main hotel hotspots of the Embarcadero, Fisherman's Wharf, Nob Hill and – most popular of all – Union Square. The latter is the most problematic for tourists looking for competitive accommodation as many hotels advertise themselves as being in the Union Square district while they are squarely located in the adjacent, less-than-desirable Tenderloin; steer clear of any 'Union Square' hotel that is located west of Taylor and south of Post.

San Francisco's temperate climate means that there is always some demand for hotel space, but the city's most popular season is spring through to late autumn, with many hotels adjusting their prices according to seasonal demand. All hotels charge 14 per cent tax on each room.

HOTELS
Beresford Arms £–££ Affiliated to the Hotel Beresford (see opposite), this boutique hotel has a slightly grander interior than its

PRICE CATEGORIES
The following categories reflect the cost of a double room per night (excluding tax).
£ up to $100   **££** $100–200   **£££** over $200

The Beresford Arms – grande dame and boutique beauty

counterpart, with similar priced rooms and amenities (including free internet access, breakfast and wine). Its proximity to the Tenderloin may deter those of a delicate disposition, but it's a bargain for those looking for a central base. ⓐ 701 Post St (Downtown) ⓣ (415) 673-2600 ⓦ www.beresford.com/arms ⓝ BART/Muni metro to Powell Street

Hotel Beresford £–££ A couple of blocks north of the bustle of Union Square and surrounded by art galleries and decent restaurants, this ornate boutique hotel offers clean, cosy rooms at competitive rates. Queen rooms include a free continental breakfast and complimentary wine and cheese in the evenings. ⓐ 635 Sutter St (Downtown) ⓣ (415) 673-9900 ⓦ www.beresford.com/beresford ⓝ BART/Muni metro to Powell Street

Red Victorian Bed & Breakfast and Peace Center £–££ With its 18 peace, love and nature-themed rooms, the Red Vic is a temple to the hippie movement in the heart of Haight Ashbury. ⓐ 1665 Haight St (The Central Districts) ⓣ (415) 864-1978 ⓦ www.redvic.com Ⓝ Muni metro: N line to Cole and Carl; Muni bus: 7, 71 to Haight and Cole

Hotel Stratford ££ It's difficult to get more central than this boutique hotel located in the heart of the Downtown retail district. Double, twin and queen rooms are spartan and simple but clean and bright, and those at the front of the premises get the benefit of the sight and sounds of the cable car running up Powell Street. ⓐ 242 Powell St (Downtown) ⓣ (415) 397-7080 ⓦ www.hotelstratford.com Ⓝ BART/Muni metro to Powell Station

King George Hotel ££ Located on the cusp of Union Square and the Tenderloin, this boutique hotel offers competitively priced accommodation in an unbeatable location. The basic rooms come with few frills, but are clean and include complimentary internet access. ⓐ 334 Mason St (Downtown) ⓣ (415) 781-5050 ⓦ www.kinggeorge.com Ⓝ BART/Muni metro to Powell Station

Laurel Inn ££ A snazzy boutique hotel in Pacific Heights offering colourful, comfortable rooms at half the price of comparable Downtown hotels. The surrounding neighbourhood provides plenty of dining and drinking options. Rates include free continental breakfast. ⓐ 444 Presidio Ave (The Central Districts) ⓣ (415) 567-8467 ⓦ www.jdvhotels.com/laurel_inn Ⓝ Muni bus: 1, 2, 3 or 43 to Presidio Avenue

Queen Anne Hotel £££ With its gorgeous Victorian architecture, opulent lobby and breakfast room and decorous bedrooms, this hotel is a gem. Guests get a full breakfast, free internet access, complimentary newspapers, a free tea-and-sherry happy hour each evening and even a gratis limousine service to anywhere in the city during weekdays. ⓐ 1590 Sutter St (The Central Districts) ⓣ (415) 441-2828 ⓦ www.queenanne.com ⓝ Bus: 38 line to Geary and Gough

HOSTELS

Green Tortoise £–££ Perched on a hill in the heart of North Beach, this cheap and cheerful hostel's accommodation comprises single beds in either female or mixed-sex dorms, private double rooms and twin rooms. Amenities include free internet connection, free breakfast of do-it-yourself pancakes and coffee and a free sauna. Reservations are strongly advised and guests are required to produce a non-California ID upon check-in. ⓐ 494 Broadway (Downtown) ⓣ (415) 834-1000 ⓦ www.greentortoise.com ⓝ BART/Muni metro to Montgomery Station, then Muni bus 9X, 9AX, or 9BX to Kearny and Broadway

USA Hostel £–££ This friendly backpacker joint is probably the best value in and around Union Square. Guests get free wireless internet access, free breakfast, coffee and tea and access to a TV lounge and games room. ⓐ 711 Post St (Downtown) ⓣ (415) 440-5600 ⓦ www.usahostels.com ⓝ BART/Muni metro to Powell Station

THE BEST OF SAN FRANCISCO

Whether you're in San Francisco for a long weekend or
a leisurely break, the City by the Bay offers a host of sights,
sounds and experiences that you simply won't find
anywhere else in the world.

TOP 10 ATTRACTIONS

- **Hire a bike** and strike out across the Golden Gate Bridge
  towards Sausalito for some stunning Bay views (see
  page 32)

- **Alcatraz** Hop aboard with the tourist hoards and take a
  ferry out to see the cells of Al Capone and other infamous
  detainees of 'The Rock' (see page 58)

- **M.H. de Young Museum** While away an entire afternoon
  admiring the formidable collection of American art
  (see page 97)

- **Ferry Building** Take a stroll through the one-time ferry
  terminal to experience the kaleidoscope of Northern
  Californian cuisine that makes San Francisco such
  a foodies' paradise (see page 64)

- **Mission District** Grab a *burrito* at one of the dozens of taquerias here and take a tour of Mission Dolores, the oldest building in the city (see page 82)

- **Land's End trail** Leave the city behind with a bracing stroll and breathtaking views of the Golden Gate and the Pacific (see page 97)

- **North Beach** Treat your senses to an evening of (Italian) wine, (loose) women, and (jazz-inspired) song at the restaurants, strip clubs, and music venues of Little Italy (see page 64)

- **AT&T Park** Feast on expensive hotdogs and stunning views of the Bay – and maybe even watch the odd inning of baseball – at the city's pristine ballpark (see page 32)

- **Anchor Brewing Company** Take a guided tour of the city's oldest brewery, then sample its wares, including the famous 'Steam' beer (see page 58)

- **Haight Ashbury** Expand your mind with a stroll through the centre of the hippie movement and a modern-day counterculture mecca (see page 82)

The city skyline at dusk

Suggested itineraries

HALF-DAY: SAN FRANCISCO IN A HURRY

Join the queue at the cable car turnaround at the intersection of Powell and Market, pay your fare and ride the rails to Fisherman's Wharf (see page 65), taking in Union Square, a sliver of Chinatown, and a great view of the Golden Gate Bridge en route.

1 DAY: TIME TO SEE A LITTLE MORE

After filling up on bagels and coffee at **Noah's Bagels** (ⓐ 100 Bush St ⓣ (415) 433-9682 ⓦ www.noahs.com), take the cable car from Downtown to Fisherman's Wharf and then catch the ferry to Alcatraz (see page 58). Once back on dry land, grab a bowl of clam chowder before taking the F Line back to the Ferry Building (see page 64). Then hit one of the happy hours on 2nd Street. After sprucing up, take the BART out to the Mission for a night of dinner and dancing.

2–3 DAYS: TIME TO SEE MUCH MORE

If it's your first time in San Francisco, allocate one day to the Fisherman's Wharf/Alcatraz/Embarcadero loop, maybe with a detour to Coit Tower (see page 62). In the evening, wander up to North Beach for some great Italian food and live music. Dedicate the next day to getting out of the tourist loop: hop on the Muni metro to Golden Gate Park, where you can hike, rent a boat, tour the Botanical Garden (see page 96), or check out the magnificent M.H. de Young Museum (see page 97). Spend your last morning wandering around the Union Square retail district, join a free guided tour of Haight Ashbury or the Castro, then take the BART back into Downtown to round the day off in style with dinner on the Embarcadero.

LONGER: ENJOYING SAN FRANCISCO TO THE FULL

Having cherry-picked from the ideas above, take in a concert at The Fillmore (see page 31), a show at the ACT (see page 67), a baseball game at AT&T Park or an American football match at Candlestick Park (see page 32).

⬛ Boats moored at Fisherman's Wharf

Something for nothing

There's plenty to do in San Francisco without spending a dime. Many of the city's smaller museums, including the **Cable Car Museum** (🚉 1201 Mason St 🕾 (415) 474-1887 🌐 www.cablecarmuseum.org) and the **San Francisco Fire Department Museum** (🚉 655 Presidio Ave 🕾 (415) 563-4630 🌐 www.sffiremuseum.org) offer free admission. Among the best no-cost resources in the city are the San Francisco City Guides Walking Tours (see page 136), which are coordinated by the San Francisco public library and conducted by local volunteer enthusiasts. Tours include everything from the history of the Gold Rush to the making of Chinatown and the Victorian Houses of Haight Ashbury. For those interested in beer making (or at least beer drinking), the Anchor Brewing Company (see page 58) offers complimentary tours of its brewery, complete with free tastings; due to the popularity of this tour, advance reservations are advisable. For a break from the city, the San Francisco Botanical Garden in Golden Gate Park (see page 96) offers free walking tours every day and twice daily at the weekends. There are also plenty of options for those who want to strike out on their own: the Land's End trail (see page 97) is a stunning way to see the Golden Gate Bridge, the Marin Headlands and the Pacific, while Golden Gate Park itself (see page 92) offers a maze of hiking trails and picnic spots. With its diverse population and many colourful characters, San Francisco is a perfect place for people watching: one of the best ways to spend a sunny day in the city is to hike to the top of Dolores Park in the Mission District with a picnic, meet the locals and take in the fabulous city views. Seasonal free highlights include the Chinatown night market fair in Portsmouth Square (see page 62) which takes place every Saturday night between July and October, and the Ferry Building Night Market (see page 64), every Thursday night between May and October.

The windmill in Golden Gate Park

When it rains

While much of San Francisco's charm is found out of doors, there's also plenty to do when it rains. Several of the city's museums, including the M.H. de Young (see page 97), the Museum of Modern Art and the Asian Art Museum (see page 68), can easily take up an entire afternoon each. Even the smaller museums, such as the Museum of the African Diaspora (see page 68), have plenty to keep visitors occupied for several hours.

Shopaholics can take advantage of bad weather to attack the expanded Westfield San Francisco Center on Market Street (see page 69). The mall offers everything from luxury department stores to a well-stocked food court to a nine-screen multiplex cinema. For the purely entertainment-minded, a good place to take refuge is the Yerba Buena Center in South of Market (see page 69). This huge complex houses a 16-screen cinema complete with an IMAX theatre, a ten-pin bowling alley, an ice-skating rink and a selection of restaurants and bars to keep you busy until the skies clear. For high-brow indoor diversion, head over to the **San Francisco Main Library** (ⓐ 100 Larkin St ⓣ (415) 557-4400 ⓦ http://sfpl.lib.ca.us), which offers free internet access, newspapers, magazines, exhibitions and (of course) a fantastic range of books. Coffee shops and bookshops (often in the same place) also provide a good place to sit and read (US book stores are full of people reading books they never buy, so don't hesitate to go native). Finally, if you're really stuck for something to do indoors, follow the example of lots of San Francisco residents and take the BART over to the East Bay, where the weather is nearly always sunnier and warmer than in the city.

● *Museum of Modern Art – a must-visit, whatever the weather*

On arrival

TIME DIFFERENCE

San Francisco follows Pacific Standard Time (PST) during the winter months, putting it eight hours behind GMT. From the second Sunday in March to the first Sunday in November, California puts the clocks forward by one hour and adjusts to Pacific Daylight Time (PDT).

ARRIVING

By air

Most international and domestic flights arrive into **San Francisco International Airport** (SFO, ⓐ PO Box 8097, San Francisco ⓣ (800) 435-9736 ⓦ www.flysfo.com), which is located about 24 km (15 miles) south of Downtown. Transfer to the city is by BART, taxi, or door-to-door shuttle bus. Signs for ground transportation and the airport BART station, which must be reached by the complimentary AirTrain, are clearly posted at the arrivals terminal. Less commonly, visitors can fly into **Oakland International Airport** (ⓐ 1 Airport Dr, Oakland ⓣ (510) 563-3300 ⓦ www.flyoakland.com) on the outskirts of Oakland. From here, visitors can take the AirBART shuttle bus to the BART Coliseum/Oakland Airport station. This runs every ten minutes from 05.00 until 00.00 (08.00 till 00.00 on Sundays). From the station, the BART takes around 20 minutes to Downtown San Francisco.

By rail

San Francisco is not directly connected to the **Amtrak**

⬤ *A taxi ride can be a whistle-stop education*

......................POI	
Ⓜ ...Metro and/or BART Stop	
✝ ....Cathedral	
ℹ️ ....Information	
🚓 ....Police Station	
✈ ....Airport	
🚊 ....Railway Stn	
🚌 ....Bus Station	
✚ ....Hospital	

San Francisco

0   500 metres
0   500 yards

Pacific Ocean

PRESIDIO

Presidio National Park

PRESIDIO HEIGHTS

South Bay

Baker Beach

China Beach

Lands End

Palace of the Legion of Honor

SEACLIFF

Lincoln Park

CALIFORNIA   STREET

GEARY   BOULEVARD

CENTRAL RICHMOND

OUTER RICHMOND

BALBOA   STREET

FULTON   STREET

Golden Gate Municipal Golf Course

Golden Gate Park

Stow Lake

LINCOLN   WAY

Ocean Beach

COLE VALLEY

SUNSET DISTRICT

GOLDEN GATE HEIGHTS

TWIN PEAKS PARK

OUTER SUNSET

NORIEGA   STREET

N

CENTRAL WEST

FOREST HILL

TARAVAL   STREET

GOLDEN GATE BRIDGE

GOLDEN GATE BRIDGE FREEWAY

OLD MASON STREET

DOYLE DRIVE

LINCOLN BOULEVARD

LINCOLN BLVD

PARK PRESIDIO BY-PASS DRIVE

STANYAN STREET

JOHN F. KENNEDY DRIVE

CROSS OVER DRIVE

LINCOLN   WAY

19TH   AVENUE

7TH   STREET

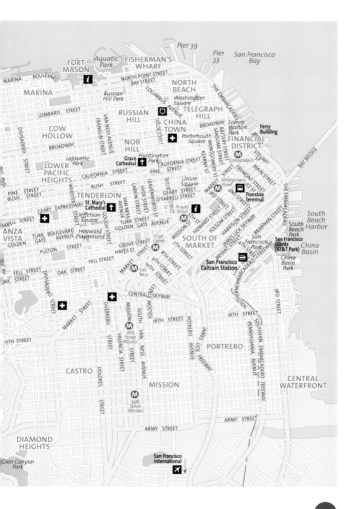

(ⓣ (800) 872-7245 ⓦ www.amtrak.com) national rail network. The nearest Amtrak station is across the Bay at **Emeryville Station** (ⓐ 5885 Horton St, Emeryville). There is no direct connection to San Francisco from Emeryville Station and passengers will need to take the free **Emery-Go-Round shuttle** (ⓣ (510) 451-3862 ⓦ www.emerygoround.com) to MacArthur BART station to get into the city. Other Amtrak stations in the Bay Area include the un-staffed, machine-only **Richmond Station** (ⓐ 1700 Nevin Ave, Richmond ⓝ BART to Richmond station) and **Oakland Jack London Square Station** (ⓐ 245 Second St, Oakland ⓝ BART to Coliseum/Oakland Airport), both of which offer direct BART connections into San Francisco. Passengers can buy tickets either at the station or aboard Amtrak trains, but the latter are more expensive. The Caltrain system offers a regional connection between San Francisco and the town of Gilroy in the South Bay with stops at Redwood City, Stanford and San Jose. Trains leave from the **San Francisco Caltrain Station** (ⓐ 4th St ⓣ (800) 660-4287 ⓦ www.caltrain.com ⓝ Muni metro: N line to Caltrain Depot). Caltrain fares are determined by a zoning system and tickets should be bought prior to travel (they are not available on board the train).

By road

Visitors arriving in San Francisco by Greyhound Bus Lines arrive at the **Transbay Terminal** (ⓐ 425 Mission St ⓣ (415) 495-1569 ⓦ www.greyhound.com ⓝ Most in-bound Muni buses) in South of Market. From here, passengers can connect to most city bus lines or walk one block north then one block east on Market Street to Embarcadero station to connect with the BART and

Muni metro services. For those arriving in the city by car, there are three main entry points: driving from the south, Highway 101 and interstate I-280 will take you directly into Downtown; from the east, cars enter the city via the San Francisco Bay Bridge (I-80), which charges a $4 toll for all in-bound traffic; and from the north, the only route into the city is the Golden Gate Bridge (Highway 101), which charges a toll of $5 for all in-bound traffic. Parking in San Francisco is in notoriously short supply and daily rates for parking garages in Downtown of around $30 reflect this. Public metered parking spaces are difficult to find and have strict time limits and high rates. Traffic in Downtown San Francisco is usually stop-and-go during the day, with bottlenecks occurring at both the morning and evening rush hours on weekdays. One particular area to avoid between the hours of 15.00 and 19.00 is the intersection of Bush and Market Streets, which is the main access point for the Financial District traffic en route to the Bay Bridge.

ORIENTATION

Thanks to some catastrophic urban planning, Downtown San Francisco operates on two grid systems that abut each other on a 45° angle. The street that divides the two grids is Market Street, which runs southwest from the Ferry Building (see page 64). Directly to the north of the easternmost end of Market Street is the Financial District, bounded by Kearny to the west and Broadway to the north. West of the Financial District is the Union Square retail district, which blends into the Tenderloin west of Taylor Street. Chinatown and North Beach are just northwest of the Financial District and Union Square, with the southern boundary of North Beach marked by the distinctively

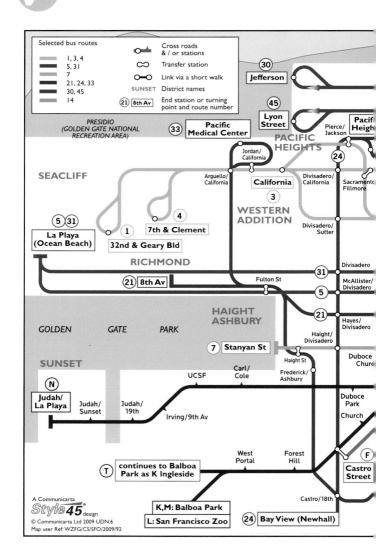

Selected bus routes

	1, 3, 4
	5, 31
	7
	21, 24, 33
	30, 45
	14

Cross roads & / or stations

Transfer station

Link via a short walk

SUNSET District names

(21) 8th Av End station or turning point and route number

(30) Jefferson

(45) Lyon Street

Pierce/ Jackson

Pacif Heigh

(24)

PRESIDIO
(GOLDEN GATE NATIONAL RECREATION AREA)

(33) Pacific Medical Center

PACIFIC HEIGHTS

Jordan/ California

SEACLIFF

Arguello/ California

California (3)

Divisadero/ California

Sacramento Fillmore

WESTERN ADDITION

(5) (31)

(1)

(4) 7th & Clement

La Playa (Ocean Beach)

32nd & Geary Bld

Divisadero/ Sutter

RICHMOND

Divisadero

(21) 8th Av

Fulton St

(31)

McAllister/ Divisadero

(5)

HAIGHT ASHBURY

(21)

Hayes/ Divisadero

GOLDEN   GATE   PARK

(7) Stanyan St

Haight/ Divisadero

SUNSET

UCSF

Carl/ Cole

Haight St

Frederick/ Ashbury

Duboce Chure

(N)

Judah/ La Playa

Judah/ Sunset

Judah/ 19th

Irving/9th Av

Duboce Park

Church

West Portal

Forest Hill

(F)

(T) continues to Balboa Park as K Ingleside

Castro Street

Castro/18th

K,M: Balboa Park

L: San Francisco Zoo

(24) Bay View (Newhall)

A Communicarta
Style45 design
© Communicarta Ltd 2009 UDN.6
Map user Ref: WZFG/CS/SFO/2009/92

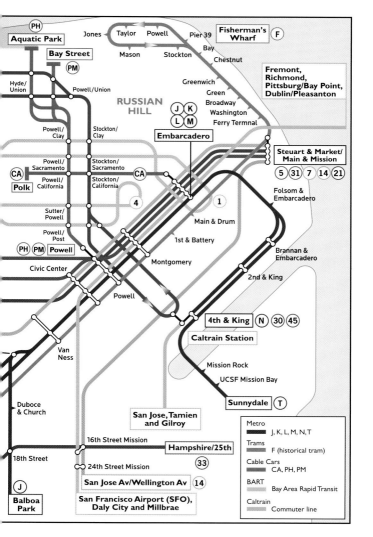

triangular Transamerica Building at 600 Montgomery Street.
The Embarcadero runs around the northeastern edge of the city
from the Ferry Building to Fisherman's Wharf. The area to the
south of Market Street is known (unsurprisingly) as South of
Market or SOMA.

GETTING AROUND

The good news for the true pedestrian urban explorer is that
Downtown San Francisco is largely accessible on foot, although
some steep inclines, such as those up to Nob Hill and Russian Hill,
can wind even the fittest of walkers and prove quite humiliating
for Joe or Josephine Average – so don't attempt anything
'because it's there'.

San Francisco benefits from one of the best public transport
systems in the country, with several efficient transit mediums.
Numbered buses and trolleybuses operated by the San Francisco
Municipal Railway, or **Muni** (ⓦ www.sfmta.com), are frequent,
reliable and inexpensive, travelling to most destinations in the
city. Muni also runs six metro lines (J, K, L, M, N and T), which are
a mixture of underground and above- ground train lines. Line F is
a tram, or historic streetcar, which travels through Market Street
between Castro and Fisherman's Wharf. A single ticket on any
Muni line, usually bought as you board the vehicle (exact fare
only), allows you to transfer to other Muni transport systems
within a 90-minute timeframe.

Another good option is the Bay Area Rapid Transit system, or
BART (ⓦ www.bart.gov), which provides fast, reliable connections
between Downtown and the Mission district as well as to the
airport, the south of San Francisco and cities in the East Bay.

⬥ *Use the cable cars for getting up those steep hills*

BART tickets must be purchased prior to travel from machines located in BART stations. There are various interconnections between BART and the Muni metro and bus lines.

In addition to all this, there are of course the three iconic cable car lines to help you beat those hills: Powell-Hyde, Powell-Mason and California.

CAR HIRE

Rental cars can be picked up at San Francisco and Oakland airports or in Downtown San Francisco. Major car rental companies in the city include:

Avis ⓐ 675 Post St ⓣ (415) 885-5011 ⓦ www.avis.com
Ⓜ BART/Muni metro to Powell St station
Enterprise ⓐ 1133 Van Ness Ave ⓣ (415) 441-3369
ⓦ www.enterprise.com Ⓜ Muni metro to Van Ness station;
Muni bus: 38, 47 to Geary and Van Ness
National ⓐ 320 O'Farrell St ⓣ (415)292-5300
ⓦ www.nationalcar.com Ⓜ BART/Muni metro to
Powell St station

▶ *A fine example of French renaissance architecture: the majestic City Hall*

THE CITY OF
San Francisco

Downtown

Located on the northeastern side of the peninsula, Downtown San Francisco and its surrounding districts encompass the commercial heart of the city as well as many of its most recognisable landmarks and visitor attractions, including Union Square, the Ferry Building, North Beach and Fisherman's Wharf.

SIGHTS & ATTRACTIONS

Alcatraz

The famous prison island and sometime home of Al Capone is a must-see destination for first-time visitors to San Francisco. Ferries leave from the mainland at Pier 33 throughout the day and provide an excellent view of the San Francisco skyline during the 20-minute crossing. Once on the island, visitors can rent audio headsets for a self-guided tour of the former penitentiary. Advance reservations are recommended through **Alcatraz Cruises** (ⓐ Pier 33, Hornblower Alcatraz Landing ❶ (415) 981-7625 ⓦ www.alcatrazcruises.com).

Anchor Brewing Company

The makers of San Francisco's famous Anchor Stream beer offer free 45-minute tours of its brewery to those interested in the production process or those who just want a couple of gratis pints. Visitors are advised to make reservations at least a month in advance. ⓐ 1705 Mariposa St ❶ Reservations: (415) 863-8350

❶ *Alcatraz – somehow stark, even in the evening sunshine*

Downtown

0 — 500 metres
0 — 500 yards

POI
Metro and/or BART Stop
Cathedral
Information
Police Station
Airport
Railway Stn
Bus Station
Hospital

San Francisco Bay

Alcatraz

Pier 33

Pier 29

Pier 39

Pier 45

Aquatic Park

THE EMBARCADERO

Ferry Building

Federal Reserve Bank

STEUART STREET

Golden Gate Center / Sidney Walton Park

Maritime Plaza

Embarcadero Center

DRUMM ST

DAVIS STREET

FRONT STREET

BATTERY STREET

SANSOME STREET

FINANCIAL DISTRICT

Pacific Heritage Museum

Bank of America

MONTGOMERY

KEARNY ST

CALIFORNIA ST

SACRAMENTO STREET

CLAY STREET

WASHINGTON STREET

JACKSON STREET

PACIFIC AVENUE

BROADWAY

Levi Strauss Building

Colt Tower

TELEGRAPH HILL

NORTH BEACH

Chinese Historical Society Museum

Club Fugazi

Washington Square

GRANT AVENUE

UNION STREET

GREEN STREET

VALLEJO STREET

FILBERT STREET

GREENWICH STREET

LOMBARD STREET

CHESTNUT STREET

COLUMBUS AVENUE

STOCKTON STREET

POWELL STREET

MASON STREET

TAYLOR STREET

JONES STREET

LEAVENWORTH STREET

HYDE STREET

LARKIN STREET

POLK STREET

VAN NESS AVENUE

CHINA TOWN

Cable Car Museum

Grace Cathedral

Huntington

NOB HILL

RUSSIAN HILL

Russian Hill Park

San Francisco Art Institute

NORTH POINT STREET

Northpoint Center

FISHERMAN'S WHARF

JEFFERSON STREET

BEACH STREET

BAY STREET

FRANCISCO STREET

The Aquarium of the Bay

Musée Mechanique

U.S.S. Pampanito

Fisherman's & Seamen's Chapel

Eureka

Balclutha

Museum of the City of San Francisco

National Maritime Museum

MONTGOMERY STREET

ⓦ www.anchorbrewing.com ⓛ Tours 13.00–15.00 Mon–Fri by reservation only ⓝ Muni bus: 22 to 17th/DeHaro St or 19 to 18th St/Rhode Island St

Chinatown

The second-largest Chinatown in the United States comprises a bustling residential and commercial area. Visitors can pick up everything from clothes and cut-price jewellery to herbs, spices, tea and suspect ivory and jade sculptures. Chinatown also offers a wealth of eating options including very reasonable dim sum restaurants. Being a living, breathing Chinatown, the area also has fresh food stores, with many ingredients so fresh that they are still alive in cages. From 18.00 to 23.00 every Saturday night from late July to late October, Chinatown's Portsmouth Square plays host to a night market fair, complete with dancers, fortune tellers and food vendors. ⓐ Stockton St & Clay St ⓦ www.sanfranciscochinatown.com ⓝ BART/Muni metro to Powell St, then Muni bus: 9AX, 9BX, 9X, 20, 30

Coit Tower at Telegraph Hill

If you want to escape the city at street level, make your way to the northeast corner of North Beach to Kearny and Filbert, where you'll find the steps that lead up to Coit Tower, an icon of the San Francisco skyline that was bequeathed to the city by Lillie Hitchcock Coit, a city resident who had a thing for firemen. The tower, which was designed to resemble a fire-hose nozzle, offers a panoramic view taking in the Golden Gate and Bay Bridges,

ⓞ *The iconic Coit Tower*

Downtown and the Marin headlands. 1 Telegraph Hill Blvd
Muni bus: 30 & 45 to Washington Square, connecting to
number 39

Ferry Building

This restored icon of the city still operates as a ferry terminal,
but is better known as a temple to local gourmet food and
wine. From the Tuscan imports shop and the fungi emporium
to the wine merchants and Scharffenberger chocolate store,
the Ferry Building is a foodie's dream come true. Lovers of fresh
produce will have to visit on Tuesday and Saturday mornings,
when the plazas to the front and rear of the Ferry Building are
transformed into local farmers' markets. 1 Ferry Building
(415) 693-0996 www.ferrybuildingmarketplace.com
10.00–18.00 Mon–Fri, 09.00–18.00 Sat, 11.00–17.00 Sun
BART/Muni metro to Embarcadero station

North Beach

Just a few hundred yards north of the Financial District, North
Beach is home to the fabulous restaurants of San Francisco's
Little Italy, as well as a host of bars, clubs and pubs. The area
was the launching pad for the Beat Generation in the 1950s,
a counter-cultural literary movement that contained the seeds
of the hippie generation, and still retains much of its bohemian
charm. Make your way up Columbus Avenue, looking in at the
City Lights book shop (261 Columbus Ave (415) 362-8193
www.citylights.com), a landmark of the Beat literary movement.
If you feel the need for some refreshment, grab a happy-hour
beer, fill up at one of the family-run Italian restaurants that line

PRIVATELY OWNED PUBLIC OPEN SPACES

One of the lesser-known assets of Downtown San Francisco is the abundance of privately owned and maintained public spaces that provide respite from a hard day's pavement-pounding. Due to the terms of a public policy implemented in the 1980s, developers of new property in the city are required to allocate ⅑ sq m (1 sq ft) of public space per 15 sq m (50 sq ft) of commercial space. As a result, Downtown San Francisco features over a dozen publicly accessible areas that range from roof deck gardens to hotel atriums. Unsurprisingly, the commercial owners of the buildings that house these public spaces are less than forthcoming about advertising their availability, but those who look hard enough will notice street level plaques granting access. The urban retreats include a rooftop garden at 100 1st Street; a garden terrace at 150 California Street; an outdoor seating area at 525 Market Street; and a public terrace with tables and chairs at 235 2nd Street. A full list of the city's Privately Owned Public Open Spaces can be found at Ⓦ www.rebargroup.org

the streets then take in a performance at one of North Beach's intimate live-music venues. Ⓐ Columbus Ave Ⓝ BART/Muni metro to Powell St station, then Muni bus 30

Pier 39 & Fisherman's Wharf

Among the silver-painted mime artists, tap dancers and rows of tat shops selling 'Alcatraz Outpatient' t-shirts, there are a couple of worthwhile activities in San Francisco's teeming tourist hotspot. Next door to restaurants and gift shops at Pier 39, **The Aquarium of the Bay** (ⓐ The Embarcadero ⓣ (888) 732-3483 ⓦ www.aquariumofthebay.com) offers a close-up view of some of the area's more exotic marine life, including over 50 species of shark. Further north, the **Musée Mechanique** (ⓐ Pier 45 Shed A, The Embarcadero ⓣ (415) 346-2000 ⓦ www.museemechanique.org)

⬤ *Catch the sea lions basking in January and February at Pier 39*

is an entertaining arcade full of mechanical games that you can still play. Further around the waterfront, the Port Walk provides a tour through tangles of working fishing boats and a smell of the fisherman's tackle. ⓦ www.pier39.com, www.fishermanswharf.org ⓒ Cable car: Powell/Hyde line from Powell St to Fisherman's Wharf; Muni metro F line

Union Square

If a city as eccentric as San Francisco can be said to have a central point it is probably Union Square. While there are plenty of opportunities for clothes shopping in the department stores that frame the plaza on all sides, the Square itself is something of a concrete no-man's land. To get a more interesting view of the workings of San Francisco life, visitors have to explore the streets around the Square: to the north, the fringes of Chinatown teem with souvenir stores; to the northeast, the high-end retailers of Post and Sutter Streets provide plenty of places to give the credit card a workout; and to the west, the Theater District offers a collection of playhouses, galleries and cheap eateries. ⓐ Between Powell St/Geary St and Stockton St/Post St ⓝ BART/Muni metro to Powell St station

CULTURE

American Conservatory Theater (ACT)

San Francisco's preeminent theatrehouse plays host to a wide variety of home-grown and touring performances in grand neoclassical surroundings. ⓐ 405 Geary St ⓣ Box office: (415) 749-2228 ⓦ www.act-sf.org ⓝ BART/Muni metro to Powell St station

Asian Art Museum

A beautiful building housing fine examples of Chinese, Japanese, Tibetan, Persian and other Asian art. It also hosts numerous special exhibitions throughout the year. ⓐ 200 Larkin St ⓣ (415) 581-3600 ⓦ www.asianart.org ⓛ 10.00–17.00 Tues, Wed, Fri–Sun, 10.00–21.00 Thur ⓜ BART/Muni metro to Civic Center station

Museum of the African Diaspora

This museum provides a fascinating insight into African culture. Its permanent exhibits include an interactive gallery on African culinary and artistic influence, a Freedom Theater and a powerful Slavery Passages room. ⓐ 685 Mission St ⓣ (415) 358-7200 ⓦ www.moadsf.org ⓛ 11.00–18.00 Wed–Sat, 12.00–17.00 Sun ⓜ BART/Muni metro to Montgomery St or Powell St stations

San Francisco Ballet

The oldest professional ballet company in the United States, the SFB offers world-class performances. ⓐ War Memorial Opera House, 301 Van Ness Ave ⓣ Tickets and information: (415) 865-2000 ⓦ www.sfballet.org ⓛ Performances at 14.00, 19.30 or 20.00 throughout the season ⓜ BART/Muni metro to Civic Center station

San Francisco Museum of Modern Art

The jewel in the crown of San Francisco's Downtown art museums, the SFMOMA houses over 15,000 examples of 20th-century art, including paintings, sculptures, photographs and media installations. ⓐ 151 3rd St ⓣ (415) 357-4000 ⓦ www.sfmoma.org ⓛ 11.00–17.45 Mon, Tues, Fri–Sun, 11.00–20.45 Thur ⓜ BART/Muni metro to Montgomery St or Powell St stations

Yerba Buena Center for the Arts

Located in the trendy South of Market area just across the road from the SFMOMA, the Yerba Buena Center is a forum for theatre, dance and other exhibitions, including art and sculpture. 🅰 701 Mission St ☎ (415) 978-2700 🌐 www.ybca.org 🕐 12.00–17.00 Tues & Wed, Fri & Sat, 12.00–20.00 Thur Ⓜ BART/Muni metro to Montgomery St or Powell St stations

RETAIL THERAPY

As San Francisco's main retail district, the area around Union Square offers an array of options. On the Square itself, **Saks Fifth Avenue** (🅰 220 Post St ☎ (415) 986-4300 🌐 www.saksfifthavenue.com), **Neiman Marcus** (🅰 150 Stockton St ☎ (415) 362-3900 🌐 www.neimanmarcus.com) and **Macy's** (🅰 170 O'Farrell St ☎ (415) 397-3333 🌐 www.macys.com) cater to all your classier department-store needs, while the boutiques of Maiden Lane offer a more individual experience. To the east of Union Square, a cluster of designer clothing flagship stores, including those of Lacoste, Thomas Pink, Coach and Prada, line the streets. If you don't fancy shopping in the great outdoors, the **Westfield San Francisco Center** (🅰 865 Market St ☎ (415) 512-6766 🌐 http://westfield.com/sanfrancisco), two blocks south of Union Square on Market Street, offers its own mix of luxury department stores (Bloomingdales and Nordstrom) as well as outlets for nearly every major American clothing brand. For a less hectic shopping experience, check out the **Crocker Galleria** (🅰 50 Post St ☎ (415) 393-1505 🌐 www.shopatgalleria.com), a mixture of boutique retailers, pampering services such as massage and nail salons, jewellery and ceramics stores. On the top floor there is a collection of lunch spots under a domed glass roof. There is also a farmers' market every Thursday selling locally grown produce.

TAKING A BREAK

Boudin Bakery £ ❶ Taste some traditional San Francisco sourdough bread with one of the famous clam chowder bread bowls or a sandwich: the turkey and cranberry sourdough baguette comes highly recommended. ❷ 619 Market St ❸ (415) 281-8200 ❿ www.boudinbakery.com 🕐 11.30–21.30 Mon–Fri, 11.00–21.00 Sat & Sun Ⓝ BART/Muni metro to Montgomery St station

Caffe Trieste £ ❷ A fixture of North Beach for generations, this neighbourhood coffee shop is a good spot to meet the modern-day locals and see portraits of some of Little Italy's famous historical characters. ❷ 601 Vallejo St ❸ (415) 392-6739 🕐 06.30–00.00 Fri & Sat, 06.30–22.00 Sun–Thur Ⓝ Muni bus: 9, 20 or 41

Landmark @ One Market £ ❸ A huge indoor space that provides a nice oasis with high ceilings, public seating and an extensive food court. On weekdays it's a great place to soak up the lunchtime buzz with the suits. ❷ 1 Market St 🕐 08.00–17.00 Mon–Fri Ⓝ BART/Muni metro to Embarcadero station

Ferry Building ££ ❹ Sit down at one of the sandwich shops or high-end snack bars inside (champagne at the Tsar Nicoulai Caviar shop is particularly recommended) or build your own picnic from the gourmet deli stores. ❷ 1 Ferry Building ❸ (415) 693-0996

🌐 www.ferrybuildingmarketplace.com 🕐 10.00–18.00 Mon–Fri, 09.00–18.00 Sat, 11.00–17.00 Sun Ⓜ BART/Muni metro to Embarcadero station

Westin St Francis ££ ❺ One of the only buildings in Downtown to survive the 1906 earthquake, this hotel provides a nice insight into 19th-century San Francisco. The café on the western end of the lobby is a nice place to take the weight off your feet, drinking a cup of coffee and listening to the resident pianist. ⓐ 335 Powell St ⓣ (415) 397-7000 🌐 www.westinstfrancis.com 🕐 06.00–22.00 Ⓜ BART/Muni metro to Powell St station

AFTER DARK

RESTAURANTS
Naan and Curry £ ❻ A curry house that serves generous portions of good, honest fare. Bring your own beer. ⓐ 336 O'Farrell St ⓣ (415) 346-1443 🕐 10.00–04.00 Ⓜ BART/Muni metro to Powell St station

Biscuits and Blues ££ ❼ A great place to take in some live music while tucking into down-home Southern cuisine. Typical menu items include corn shrimp fritters. ⓐ 401 Mason St ⓣ (415) 292-2583 🌐 www.biscuitsandblues.com 🕐 18.00–23.30 Ⓜ BART/Muni metro to Powell St station

The Stinking Rose ££ ❽ A restaurant devoted entirely to garlic. Dishes include 40-clove garlic chicken, garlic hummus cocktail and garlic ice cream. Check out the gift shop on the way out.

ⓐ 325 Columbus Ave ⓣ (415) 781-7673 ⓦ www.thestinkingrose.com
ⓛ 11.00–23.00 ⓜ BART/Muni metro to Montgomery St station

Chaya Brasserie £££ ⓽ This trendy Asian-fusion restaurant
includes a sit-down restaurant and a separate sushi bar, both
with fab food and great views of the Bay. The nightly sushi happy
hour (17.30 to 19.30) is a good deal. ⓐ 132 The Embarcadero
ⓣ (415) 777-8688 ⓦ www.thechaya.com ⓛ 11.30–14.00 Mon–Fri,
17.30–22.00 Mon–Wed & Sun, 17.30–22.30 Thur–Sat ⓜ BART/Muni
metro to Embarcadero station

Osha Thai £££ ⓾ Located opposite the Ferry Building, this
trendy restaurant serves up generous portions of Thai and Asian-
fusion cuisine at half the price of other Embarcadero eateries.
ⓐ 4 The Embarcadero ⓣ (415) 788-6742 ⓦ www.oshathai.com/4
ⓛ 11.00–00.00 ⓜ BART/Muni metro to Embarcadero station

Ozumo £££ ⑪ One of the most expensive Japanese restaurants
in the city, Ozumo has sashimi to die for and a wide range of
inventive fusion plates. It also offers an impressive range of
sakes. ⓐ 161 Steuart St ⓣ (415) 882-1333 ⓦ www.ozumo.com
ⓛ 11.30–14.00 Mon–Fri, 17.30–22.30 Mon–Thur, 17.30–23.00 Fri & Sat,
17.30–22.00 Sun ⓜ BART/Muni metro to Embarcadero station

Plouf £££ ⑫ Pricey Parisian-style bistro that's known for
its fabulous French-style fish dishes and its friendly staff.
ⓐ 40 Belden Pl, off Bush St ⓣ (415) 986-6491 ⓦ www.ploufsf.com
ⓛ 11.30–15.00 Mon–Fri, 17.30–22.00 Mon–Thur, 17.30–23.00 Fri &
Sat ⓜ BART/Muni metro to Montgomery St station; Muni bus: 9X

⬥ *Seafood platters typify one aspect of the city's cuisine*

Shanghai 1930 £££ ⓭ An ultra-chic subterranean Chinese restaurant featuring live music and a happy hour on weeknights. Favourites such as wonton and spring rolls share the menu with more adventurous fusion dishes, including the highly recommended sesame profiteroles. ⓐ 133 Steuart St ⓣ (415) 896-5600 ⓦ www.shanghai1930.com ⓛ 11.30–14.30 Mon–Fri, 17.30–22.00 Mon–Thur, 17.30–23.00 Fri & Sat ⓝ BART/Muni metro to Embarcadero station

Slanted Door £££ ⓮ With great views over the Bay and an uber-stylish cocktail-sipping clientele, this Ferry Building restaurant offers delicious (and beautifully presented) Californian-Vietnamese dishes. ⓐ 1 Ferry Building ⓣ (415) 861-8032 ⓦ www.slanteddoor.com ⓛ 11.00–14.30, 17.30–22.00 ⓝ BART/Muni metro to Embarcadero station

Tadich Grill £££ ⓯ This 150-year-old seafood restaurant is a legacy of Barbary Coast times. The place is packed for lunch most weekdays, but its crab cakes are worth waiting for. ⓐ 240 California St ⓣ (415) 391-1849 ⓛ 11.00–21.30 Mon–Fri, 11.30–21.30 Sat ⓝ BART/Muni metro to Embarcadero station

Teatro Zinzanni £££ ⓰ As much an extravaganza as a dining experience, this unique venue promises 'Love, Chaos and Dinner'. Performers include jugglers, magicians and cabaret artists who entertain you while you tuck into your five-course meal. ⓐ Pier 29 ⓣ (415) 438-2668 ⓦ http://love.zinzanni.org ⓛ Show starts 18.55 Wed–Sat, doors open 18.00; show starts 17.55 Sun, doors open 17.00 ⓝ Street car: F line

PUBS & CLUBS

111 Minna Gallery An art gallery by day, this SOMA destination turns into a party venue by night, complete with a DJ, a bar and plenty of hipsters dressed to impress. @ 111 Minna St ☎ (415) 974-1719 ⓦ www.111minnagallery.com ⏰ Hours vary by exhibition, so phone or consult website to check Ⓝ BART/Muni metro to Montgomery St station

Irish Bank Formerly a bank, this charming pub has many of the old trappings of its financial heritage still hanging on the walls. Any night of the week, its outdoor courtyard plays host to the financial-district workers that cram in with pints of Guinness in hand. @ 10 Mark Lane at Bush St ☎ (415) 788-7152 ⓦ www.theirishbank.com ⏰ 11.30–02.00 Ⓝ BART/Muni metro to Montgomery St station

John Colins Rammed on weeknights, this candle-lit bar is a magnet for the South of Market after-work crew, particularly during its excellent happy hour. @ 90 Natoma St ☎ (415) 543-2277 ⓦ www.johncolins.com ⏰ 17.00–02.00 Mon–Fri, 21.00–02.00 Sat Ⓝ BART/Muni metro to Montgomery St station

One Market A favourite after-work spot for the Financial District crowd, the bar features a happy hour and some excellent nibbles. @ 1 Market St ☎ (415) 777-5577 ⏰ 11.30–21.00 Mon–Fri, 17.30–21.00 Sat Ⓝ BART/Muni metro to Embarcadero station

Schroeder's This 1930s-style Munich beer hall offers giant steins of German lager with polka dancing and beer-drinking

competitions on Friday nights. @ 240 Front St ☎ (415) 421-4778
Ⓦ www.schroederssf.com ☻ 11.00–21.00 Mon–Fri, 16.30–21.00
Sat Ⓝ BART/Muni metro to Embarcadero station

Swig This trendy urban bar in the heart of the Tenderloin is known
for its vast selection of spirits and its inviting decoration complete
with fireplace. @ 561 Geary St ☎ (415) 931-7292 Ⓦ www.swigbar.com
☻ 15.00–02.00 Ⓝ BART/Muni metro to Powell St station

Thirsty Bear Brewing Company One of a handful of San Francisco-
based breweries, the Thirsty Bear sells a range of potent microbrews
and some great bar food to soak them up. @ 661 Howard St
☎ (415) 974-0905 Ⓦ www.thirstybear.com ☻ 11.30–22.00 Mon–Thur,
11.30–00.00 Fri, 12.00–00.00 Sat, 17.00–22.00 Sun Ⓝ BART/Muni
metro to Montgomery St station

Tunnel Top A trendy hangout for the after-work crowd, this
central bar offers decent cocktails and a comfortable environment
to enjoy them in. @ 601 Bush St ☎ (415) 986-8900 ☻ 17.00–02.00
Mon–Sat Ⓝ BART/Muni metro to Montgomery St station

Vesuvio Cafe A kitsch bar in which the decor consists of multi-
coloured lamps, eclectic ornaments and anything the owners were
able to nail to the walls. @ 255 Columbus Ave ☎ (415) 362-3370
Ⓦ www.vesuvio.com ☻ 06.00–02.00 Ⓝ BART/Muni metro to
Montgomery St station

The Warfield The one-time home of San Francisco rock icons
The Grateful Dead, this popular music venue manages to

retain an intimate atmosphere while packing in 2,000 people.

🅐 982 Market St 🅣 (415) 345-1265 🅦 www.thewarfieldtheatre.com

🅛 Hours vary by event, so phone or consult website to check

🅝 BART/Muni metro to Civic Center or Powell St stations

🔺 *The kitsch delight that is Vesuvio Cafe*

The Central Districts

The residential districts in the centre of San Francisco are
the city's most vibrant and culturally diverse areas. The Latino-
dominated Mission offers great Mexican food and perhaps the
best nightlife in the city. Next door, the colourful Castro is home
to much of the city's large gay community, while Haight Ashbury,
the site of the famous Summer of Love, keeps the hippie dream
alive. The upmarket Pacific Heights district is a great place to find
boutique clothes stores and pampering services.

SIGHTS & ATTRACTIONS

Castro

The intersection of Market and Castro Streets marks the edge
of the Castro quarter, San Francisco's gay neighbourhood and
one of the most prominent pink districts in the world. Bedecked
with giant rainbow flags and packed with shops, bars and clubs
catering to the (male) gay community, the Castro is also a must-
see for anyone intending to get a true picture of the character
of modern-day San Francisco. Running south from Market,
Castro Street is at the heart of the action, and home to the
Castro Theater, a 1920s movie palace that retains its baroque
charm. The commercial centre of Castro Street runs between
Market and 19th Streets, where, among the bars and restaurants,
you'll find a number of boutique clothing, shoe and arts shops,
as well as stores catering to an exclusively gay clientele. While the
Castro is predominantly the stomping ground of gay men, the area
is generally accommodating of anyone with an open mind and

⬥ The neon-lit theatrically of the Castro area

The Central Districts

a sense of fun. www.webcastro.com Muni metro: L, M or K lines to Castro station

Haight Ashbury

The epicentre of the Summer of Love is now a bohemian refuge for modern-day hippies, amateur musicians, street-dwellers, panhandlers looking for marijuana research funding and all manner of 'off-the-grid' San Francisco denizens. Aside from the counter-cultural establishments, Haight Street offers a surprisingly wide array of independent retailers, including some chic clothing boutiques and shoe shops. Just inside the park at Haight and Stanyan, Hippie Hill attracts a colourful collection of drummers, loungers and stoners. Eating and drinking options are also plentiful. www.haightshop.com Muni bus: 6, 7 or 71

CULTURE

Mision San Francisco de Asis (Mission Dolores)

The oldest building in San Francisco is also the one that gave both the city and the surrounding district their names. The Mission comprises two main buildings: the Old Mission building, completed in 1791, and the newer Basilica, rebuilt in 1918 following the great earthquake. The entrance fee is well worth it just to get inside the adobe Old Mission with its gilded altars and ornate sanctuary. Visitors can then access the Basilica, which boasts a series of wood carvings illustrating the Seven Sorrows ('Dolores') of Mary and an impressive number of stained glass windows depicting each of the 21 California missions. 3321 16th St (415) 621-8203 www.missiondolores.org 09.00–16.30

◗ *Mission Dolores is the oldest building in San Francisco*

HIPPIEDOM'S FINAL RESTING PLACE

When tens of thousands of people converged on San Francisco for the Summer of Love in 1967, the hippie movement, which had been started by people who wanted to replace the commercialism of American life with a more communal, nature-loving philosophy (which had proved very popular), was already beginning to decline. In October 1967, a group of hippies called the Diggers, who believed themselves to embody the authentic spirit of the movement, decided to formally symbolise the death of the phenomenon with a burial ritual at Buena Vista Park. Carrying candles and parading a cardboard coffin that was supposed to contain the body of the hippie movement, they dug a hole in the grass verge at the entrance to the park on Buena Vista Avenue. A press release accompanying the ceremony announced the 'Death of Hippie, son of media and the birth of the Free Man'. For the people who had started it, the era of peace, love and rock and roll was over. What a drag.

May–Oct; 09.00–16.00 Nov–Apr ⊘ BART to 16th Street Mission. Admission charge

RETAIL THERAPY

In contrast to the chains and department stores of Union Square, the districts outside Downtown offer more intimate pockets of independent clothing and jewellery stores, as well as gift shops, handicrafts and entertainment outlets. Small commercial strips of boutique stores are found in Hayes Street in Hayes Valley, which itself contains a number of boutique clothing and shoe stores; Union Street in the Marina, which offers a mixture of high-fashion clothing, jewellers and health and beauty stores; Haight Street in Upper Haight, which has an eclectic mix of shoe shops, art stores and hippie memorabilia; and Castro Street in the Castro, which specialises in (men's) clothing, shoe shops and homeware stores. Deserving of a special mention is **Amoeba Records** (ⓐ 1855 Haight St ⓣ (415) 831-1200 ⓦ www.amoeba.com) a huge warehouse full of classic, contemporary and collector's music, including a great selection of used and new vinyl. Listening booths enable shoppers to sample the wares before buying, while regular live shows give them a chance to see some of San Francisco's up-and-coming bands in the flesh.

TAKING A BREAK

Asqew Grill £ ❶ Specialising in grilled fish, meat and vegetable skewers, this bright, colourful Cal-cuisine eatery in the middle of Haight Street is the ideal place to fill up with a tasty lunch. ⓐ 1607 Haight St ⓣ (415) 701-9301 ⓦ www.asqewgrill.com ⓛ 10.00–22.00 ⓝ Muni bus: 6 or 71

Cafe Abir £ ❷ With its free Wi-Fi, this bright, airy coffee shop is a magnet for the latte-drinking, laptop-toting crowd, and its rocket-fuel coffee and homemade sandwiches are a big draw. ⓐ 1300 Fulton St ⓣ (415) 567-6503 ⓛ 06.00–00.00 ⓝ Muni bus: 5 or 21

Mitchell's Ice Cream £ ❸ If you're a connoisseur of exotic ice-cream flavours, this is the spot for you. Mitchell's offers a great selection of tropical and delicious ice-creams, including some offbeat Filipino ones. In November, try a scoop of pumpkin with a dollop of Mexican chocolate. ⓐ 688 San Jose Ave ⓣ (415) 648-2300 ⓦ www.mitchellsicecream.com ⓛ 11.00–23.00 ⓝ Muni metro: J line to Dolores Street and 30th

Spikes £ ❹ This proudly independent coffee shop sells a large selection of coffee by the cup and by the pound. The chocolate brownies and flapjacks are highly recommended. ⓐ 4117 19th St ⓣ (415) 626-5573 ⓦ www.spikescoffee.com ⓛ 06.30–19.00 Mon–Sat, 07.30–19.00 Sun ⓝ Muni metro: F line to Castro St station

Tartine Bakery £ ❺ The perfect place to stock up on pastries and coffee before heading to Dolores Park for some sunbathing. ⓐ 600 Guerrero St ⓣ (415) 487-2600 ⓦ www.tartinebakery.com ⓛ 08.00–19.00 Mon, 07.30–19.00 Tues & Wed, 07.30–20.00 Thur & Fri, 08.00–20.00 Sat, 09.00–20.00 Sun ⓝ BART to 16th Street Mission

AFTER DARK

RESTAURANTS

Axum Cafe £ ❻ With friendly staff, no-nonsense service and great food, Axum is one of the best Ethiopian restaurants in the area. The very reasonably-priced vegetarian combo is a great way to experiment with a number of Ethiopian dishes, or the tipsy lamb

is great if you want to go solo. ⓐ 698 Haight St ⓣ (415) 252-7912
ⓦ www.axumcafe.com ⓛ 17.00–22.30 ⓝ Muni bus: 71 or 22

Puerto Alegre £ ❼ One of dozens of *taquerias* in the Mission,
this popular Mexican restaurant serves great *burritos* and *fajitas*
but even better margaritas. ⓐ 546 Valencia St ⓣ (415) 255-8201
ⓛ 11.00–22.00 Mon, 17.00–23.00 Tues, 11.00–23.00 Wed–Sun
ⓝ BART to 16th Street Mission

Cafe Gratitude ££ ❽ This vegan raw-food restaurant is a very
San Franciscan experience. All dishes on the menu have world-
affirming names and the staff will encourage you to be grateful.
To visitors, the whole celebration of aliveness can appear a little
pretentious, but the all-organic food is good. ⓐ 400 Harrison St
ⓣ (415) 824-4652 ⓦ www.cafegratitude.com ⓛ 10.00–22.00
ⓝ BART to 16th Street Mission or 24th Street Mission

Eiji £££ ❾ This unassuming and authentic Japanese
restaurant offers fabulously fresh sashimi and a great
selection of traditional and Californian-influenced sushi rolls.
ⓐ 317 Sanchez St ⓣ (415) 558-8149 ⓛ 11.30–14.00, 17.30–22.00
Tues–Sun ⓝ BART to 16th Street Mission

Nopa £££ ❿ Uber-trendy restaurant-bar with soaring
ceilings and funky murals. Drinkers can indulge in a colourful
concoction from the artisan cocktail menu, while diners enjoy
a range of Mediterranean-inspired California-fusion dishes.
ⓐ 560 Divisadero St ⓣ (415) 864-8643 ⓦ www.nopasf.com
ⓛ 17.00–01.00 ⓝ Muni bus: 24, 21, 5

⬥ *Harvey's – gay by nature and warmly inclusive*

PUBS & CLUBS

Amnesia This baroque neighbourhood favourite hosts local live music, DJs and other entertainment in plush red velveteen surroundings. ⓐ 853 Valencia St ⓣ (415) 970-0012 ⓦ www.amnesiathebar.com ⓛ 18.00–02.00 ⓝ BART to 16th Street Mission or 24th Street Mission

Elbo Room This tastefully gloomy bar and live-music venue claims to have San Francisco's longest happy hour (17.00 to 21.00 every day), complete with lethally strong cocktails. A huge range of live acts plays most nights. ⓐ 647 Valencia St ⓣ (415) 552-7788 ⓦ www.elbo.com ⓛ 17.00–02.00 ⓝ BART to 16th Street Mission

Fly Bar Grab a happy-hour half-price pizza, a pitcher of microbrewed beer or a sake cocktail and a game of pool at this hipster hang-out. ⓐ 762 Divisadero St ⓣ (415) 931-4359 ⓦ www.flybarandrestaurant.com ⓛ 17.00–02.00 Mon, 12.00–02.00 Tues–Sun ⓝ Muni bus: 24, 5, 21

Harvey's This popular spot in the heart of the Castro is named in honour of Harvey Milk, San Francisco's first openly gay prominent elected official, who was assassinated in 1978. In addition to being a noted gay cruising spot – which you might like to bear in mind if you or members of your posse are sensitive to courtship rituals – Harvey's offers extensive brunch, lunch and dinner menus, and draws a mixed clientele to its free weeknight entertainment and great nightly happy hour. ⓐ 500 Castro St ⓣ (415) 431-4278 ⓦ www.harveyssf.com

🕐 11.00–23.00 Mon–Fri, 09.00–02.00 Sat & Sun ⓦ Muni metro:
L, M or K lines to Castro station

Latin American Club Identifiable by its giant neon horseshoe
sign, this unpretentious bar is famous for its mind-blowingly
strong cocktails and its pints of Margaritas. Clear your schedule
for the following morning if you plan to spend the night here.
ⓐ 3286 22nd St ☎ (415) 647-2732 🕐 18.00–02.00 ⓦ BART to
24th Street Mission

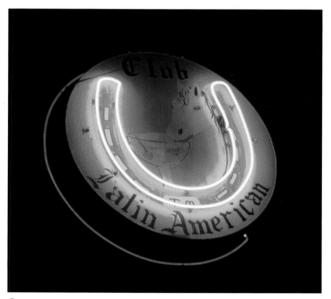

🔺 Latin American Club – where cocktails double as general anaesthetics

Mad Dog in the Fog A favourite haunt of British football fans, this sports bar serves up hand-pulled ale and Premiership matches. 🅐 530 Haight St 🕔 (415) 626-7279 🕓 11.30–02.00 Mon–Fri, 10.00–02.00 Sat & Sun 🅝 Muni bus: 22 or 71 ❶ No credit cards

Magnolia The home-brewed beers at this gastropub might be served in small glasses, but what they lack in volume they make up for in strength. 🅐 1398 Haight St 🕔 (415) 864-7468 🅦 www.magnoliapub.com 🕓 12.00–00.00 Mon–Thur, 12.00–01.00 Fri, 10.00–01.00 Sat, 10.00–23.00 Sun 🅝 Muni bus: 6, 7, 43 or 71

Medjool This swanky Middle-Eastern-themed bar and restaurant offers daily menus for lunch and dinner as well as a range of tasty bar snacks and fancy cocktails. The rooftop bar, with its great view of Downtown, is a wonderful place to be. 🅐 2522 Mission St 🕔 (415) 550-9055 🅦 www.medjoolsf.com 🕓 17.00–22.00 Mon–Thur, 17.00–02.00 Fri & Sat 🅝 BART to 24th Street Mission

Monk's Kettle This upmarket gastropub has a massive selection of world beers and some great bar snacks with suggested beer pairings and more substantial lunch and dinner options. 🅐 3141 16th St 🕔 (415) 865-9523 🅦 www.monkskettle.com 🕓 12.00–02.00 🅝 BART to 16th Street Mission

Zeitgeist A local hangout offering a range of draught brews, a nice urban beer garden and surprisingly good food cooked by tattooed foodies. 🅐 199 Valencia St 🕔 (415) 255-7505 🕓 09.00–02.00 🅝 BART to 16th Street Mission ❶ No credit cards

The West

The west of the San Francisco peninsula is dominated by Golden Gate Park and the Presidio, which offers some of the most stunning views in Northern California. The Park itself contains some of the city's most notable natural and cultural attractions, including the California Academy of Sciences and the M.H. de Young Museum. On either side, the park is flanked

THE UNLIKELY SUCCESS OF GOLDEN GATE PARK

If there is one testament to the strength of spirit and independence that embodies San Francisco, it is the miracle that is Golden Gate Park. In his 1870 survey of the area of then-barren sand dunes, the park's designer, William Hammond Hall, disregarded the advice of his peers and the prevailing wisdom of the day. With his deputy, John McLaren, Hall set forward a vision of using reclamation techniques to bring the unruly terrain into order. Lack of funding and opposition to the park from influential San Francisco businessmen who wanted to build a racetrack instead eventually prompted Hall's resignation and he passed the project onto McLaren. Over the next fifty years, McLaren coordinated an extensive planting and landscaping programme that saw the park grow from a small scrubland to a hugely popular retreat for the residents of the city. Today it is home to over one million trees and its botanical gardens boast over 7,000 species of plants.

⬤ *The Golden Gate Bridge: an obligatory backdrop for holiday snaps*

The West

Lands End
China Beach
Lands End coastal trail
SEA CLIFF
EL CAMINO DEL MAR
CALIFORNIA STREET
Lincoln Park
Palace of the Legion of Honor
EL CAMINO DEL MAR
SEA ROCK DRIVE
CLEMENT STREET
Cliff House
OUTER RICHMOND
GEARY BOULEVARD
ANZA STREET
BALBOA STREET
CABRILLO STREET
POINT LOBOS AVE
GREAT HIGHWAY
FULTON STREET
Golden Gate Municipal Golf Course
Golden Gate Park
LINCOLN WAY
UPPER GREAT HIGHWAY
LA PLAYA
IRVING STREET
JUDAH STREET
Ocean Beach
KIRKHAM STREET
SUNSET BOULEVARD
MORAGA STREET
SUNSET DISTRICT
NORIEGA STREET
OUTER SUNSET
ORTEGA STREET
PACHECO STREET

POI
Metro and/or BART Stop
Cathedral
Information
Police Station
Airport
Railway Stn
Bus Station
Hospital

by the largely forgettable districts of the Richmond and the Sunset, although both areas have small pockets of bars and restaurants that are worth visiting.

SIGHTS & ATTRACTIONS

The Botanical Garden at Strybing Arboretum
Running for ten blocks along the south side of Golden Gate Park, the Botanical Garden at Strybing Arboretum is a natural jewel in the heart of the city. Since its opening in 1940, this idyllic venue has become home to a vast selection of plants from all around the world that thrive in San Francisco's unique microclimate. Free walking tours leave from the arboretum's book store each weekday at 13.30, with extra tours at 10.30 on Saturdays and Sundays. Or just relax on one of the grassy expanses and open up a picnic and bask in the sunshine. ⓐ 9th Ave at Lincoln Way ① (415) 661-1316 ⓦ www.sfbotanicalgarden.org ⓛ 08.00–16.30 Mon–Fri, 10.00–17.00 Sat & Sun ⓝ Muni metro: N line to Irving and 9th Avenue; Muni bus: 41, 77.

California Academy of Sciences
Designed to blend in with its natural surroundings, this undulating structure contains a planetarium, aquarium and natural history museum, as well as the deepest living coral display in the world. The living roof is an 18,300 sq m (197,000 sq ft) canopy of native plants. Other highlights include the 9 m (30 ft) Foucault Pendulum, a rainforest gallery and an alligator-filled swamp. ⓐ 55 Music Concourse Dr, Golden Gate Park ① (415) 379-8000 ⓦ www.calacademy.org ⓛ 09.30–17.00 Mon–Sat, 11.00–17.00 Sun

◎ Muni metro: N line to Irving and 9th Avenue; Muni bus: 5 to Fulton and 8th Street. Admission charge

Land's End coastal trail

Running from the junction of 32nd Avenue and El Camino Del Mar in the Richmond District to the Cliff House on Ocean Beach, the Land's End hike is a must-see feature of San Francisco on a clear day. The 2.4 km (1 ½ miles) hike takes in some of the most breathtaking views of the Golden Gate Bridge, the Marin Headlands and the Pacific Ocean. If you're starting from the Richmond District end, it is worth making a detour along Sea Cliff to China Beach past some of the most expensive real estate in the city. ◎ Muni bus: 38 to Geary and 32nd Avenue

CULTURE

M.H. de Young Museum

The 'de Young' is one of San Francisco's most eye-catching (and controversial) landmarks. The structure is clad in copper gauze, which is designed to turn green through gradual oxidisation in order to blend in with its natural surroundings. In addition to its impressive series of visiting exhibitions from around the world, the museum houses a large permanent collection of North American art from the 17th to the 20th century, including pottery, sculpture, photography and paintings, as well as a large collection of Latin American, Pacific and African exhibits spanning hundreds of years. The top floor of the twisting Hamon tower is open to the public until 16.30 every day and affords spectacular views of Golden Gate Park and the city beyond. ⓐ 50 Hagiwara Tea Garden Dr,

Golden Gate Park ☎ (415) 750-3600 ⓦ www.famsf.org/deyoung
🕐 09.30–17.15 Tues–Sun (Fri until 20.45, mid-Jan–Nov) ⓝ Muni
metro: N line to Irving and 9th Avenue; Muni bus: 5 to Fulton and
8th Street. Admission charge; free on first Tues of the month

Palace of the Legion of Honor

Set between Clement Street and the Presidio, this handsome
fine-art museum is a scale imitation of the original in Paris. In
keeping with its architecture, the museum houses a collection
of European art, including casts of all of Rodin's sculptures and
works by Degas, Renoir and Picasso. ❸ Lincoln Park, 34th Ave
& Clement St ☎ (415) 750-3600 ⓦ www.famsf.org/legion
🕐 09.30–17.15 Tues–Sun ⓝ Muni bus: 18 to the Legion of
Honor. Admission charge; free on first Tues of the month

⬤ *Palace of the Legion of Honor by night*

RETAIL THERAPY

Running west of Arguello Boulevard and parallel to the Geary corridor, **Clement Street** (Muni bus: 2 to Arguello and Clement) is home to a small commercial strip featuring a number of handicraft stores, art galleries and beauty salons.

TAKING A BREAK

Crepevine £ ❶ A popular brunch destination serving up hearty crepes with a selection of sweet and savoury fillings. The California Crepe with spicy salsa is highly recommended. ❷ 624 Irving St ❶ (415) 681-5858 ❼ www.crepevine.com ❹ 07.30–23.00 Mon–Thur & Sun, 07.30–00.00 Fri & Sat ❹ Muni metro: N line to Irving and 9th Avenue

◔ *Relax in the Japanese Tea Garden at Golden Gate Park*

Java Beach £ ❷ Busy beachside café serving strong coffee, delicious sandwiches and excellent carrot cake. It also offers draught beers and free Wi-Fi. ⓐ 1396 La Playa ❶ (415) 665-5282 ⓦ www.javabeachcafe.com ⓛ 05.30–23.00 Mon–Fri, 06.00–23.00 Sat & Sun ⓝ Muni metro: N line to Judah and 48th Avenue

AFTER DARK

RESTAURANTS
Beach and Park Chalet ££ ❸ Located along the Great Highway, this restaurant and brewery gives you two for the price of one, with a beach-facing upstairs restaurant and a patio to the rear that abuts the western edge of Golden Gate Park. While the food in the restaurant is average California fare, the booze is great; if you don't know what you want, try the six-beer sampler, which is served in a wooden carousel. ⓐ 1000 Great Hwy ❶ (415) 386-8439 ⓦ www.beachchalet.com ⓛ 09.00–22.30 Mon–Thur, 09.00–23.00 Fri, 08.00–23.00 Sat, 08.00–22.00 Sun ⓝ Muni bus: 18 to The Great Highway

Burma Superstar ££ ❹ Traditional Burmese restaurant that draws people from all over the city with its tasty salads, wholesome curries and a unique dining experience. Perennial favourites include the enlivening Tea Leaf Salad and the 22-ingredient Rainbow Salad that is mixed with kaleidoscopic drama at your tableside. ⓐ 309 Clement St ❶ (415) 387-2147 ⓦ www.burmasuperstar.com ⓛ 11.00–15.30, 17.00–21.30 Sun–Thur, 11.00–15.30, 17.00–22.00 Fri & Sat ⓝ Muni bus: 2 to Clement and 4th Avenue

El Mansour ££ ⑤ Colourful Moroccan restaurant featuring an exotic menu of seafood, chicken, lamb and rabbit specialities. Diners are treated to belly dancing and elaborate tea pouring into the bargain. ⓐ 3119 Clement St ⓣ (415) 751-2312 ⓦ www.elmansour.com ⓛ 17.00–22.00 Tues–Sun ⓝ Muni bus: 2 to Clement Street and 32nd Avenue

Oyaji £££ ⑥ For an authentic *izakaya* experience in San Francisco, Oyaji takes some beating. The jovial master-san serves up a host of tasty traditional Japanese dishes, including excellent tempura. ⓐ 3123 Clement St ⓣ (415) 379-3604 ⓛ 17.30–22.30 Tues–Thur, 17.30–00.00 Fri & Sat, 17.30–22.00 Sun ⓝ Muni bus: 2 to Clement Street and 32nd Avenue

Pizzetta 211 £££ ⑦ An impossibly small pizzeria that has only four tables inside and two on the pavement; but this doesn't stop the locals from waiting for hours to get one. It specialises in thin-crust pizzas with fresh toppings and decadent desserts. ⓐ 211 23rd Ave ⓣ (415) 379-9880 ⓛ 17.00–21.00 Mon, 12.00–14.30, 17.00–21.00 Wed–Fri, 12.00–21.00 Sat & Sun ⓝ Muni bus: 2 to Clement and 23rd Avenue

PUBS & CLUBS
Bitter End A little more civilised than the Dogs Bollix across the street, the Bitter End combines an authentic pub experience with some decent pub grub options, including shepherd's pie and fish and chips and a comprehensive weekend brunch menu. Check out

● *Serving up rocket fuel at the Rockit Room*

the trivia night on Tuesdays. 408 Clement St (415) 221-9538 16.00–02.00 Mon–Fri, 11.00–02.00 Sat & Sun Muni bus: 2 to Clement Street and 4th Avenue

Little Shamrock This shabby, charming Irish drinking hole has been standing for over a hundred years and offers a good selection of beers, an interesting array of board games and a make-it-yourself popcorn machine. What more could you ask for? 807 Lincoln Way (415) 661-0060 15.00–02.00 Mon–Fri, 13.00–02.00 Sat & Sun Muni metro: N line to Irving and 9th Avenue

Pig and Whistle Tucked away from the traffic of Geary Boulevard, the 'Pig' is the nearest thing to an authentic British pub that you'll find in San Francisco. The clientele is a mixture of ex-pats and locals, the food is wholesome pub grub and there's a good selection of ales and bar games including pool and darts. Check out the quiz nights every Sunday and Wednesday. 2801 Geary Blvd (415) 885-4779 www.pig-and-whistle.com 11.30–02.00 Muni bus: 38 to Geary and Masonic

Rockit Room (406 Clement) Popular local-music venue that features a large upstairs performance area, which hosts gigs most nights of the week. Theme nights include acoustic Mondays, open-mic Tuesdays and tribute bands on other evenings. There are drinks specials most nights. 406 Clement St (415) 387-6343 www.rock-it-room.com 19.00–02.00 Muni bus: 2 to Clement and 4th Avenue

---

A sleepy yacht harbour in North Bay

Angel Island & Sausalito

About 6.5 km (4 miles) north of San Francisco, Angel Island provides welcome relief from the tourists on Alcatraz. In addition to wonderful hiking and biking trails, the island offers an insight into the military and cultural history of San Francisco, particularly through its immigration station museum. The picturesque town of Sausalito lies to the north of San Francisco and provides a great escape from the city. Perched on the waterfront, it offers a relaxed mix of restaurants, cafés and shops as well as a range of outdoor activities that take advantage of the stunning natural backdrop of the bay.

GETTING THERE

Angel Island and Sausalito can both be reached by ferry from various points of departure in San Francisco. **Blue and Gold Fleet** (Ⓔ Pier 41, Fisherman's Wharf ❶ (415) 705-5555 Ⓦ www.blueandgoldfleet.com) offers year-round departures from the Ferry Building (once daily on weekdays, twice daily on weekends) and Pier 41 in Fisherman's Wharf (twice daily on weekdays and three times daily on weekends) to Angel Island, as well as five daily return services from Pier 41 to Sausalito. **Golden Gate Ferries** (❶ (415) 455-2000 Ⓦ www.goldengateferry.org) also operates a daily service from the Ferry Building to Sausalito, leaving approximately every 90 minutes. Sausalito is reachable by Golden Gate Transit buses numbers 2, 10 and 60 from Downtown San Francisco to Bridgeway and Bay (on weekdays only).

🔺 *The mists roll in over colourful Sausalito and its hillside homes*

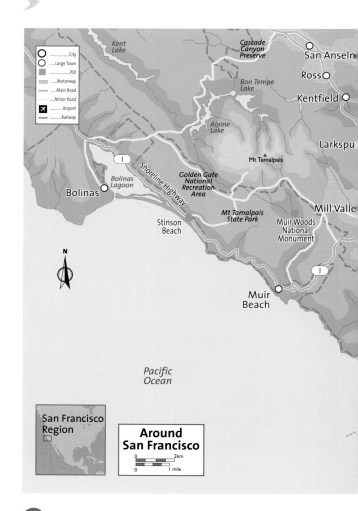

Around San Francisco

San Francisco Region

Pacific Ocean

○	City
○	Large Town
■	POI
	Motorway
	Main Road
	Minor Road
✈	Airport
	Railway

Kent Lake

Cascade Canyon Preserve

San Anseln

Bon Tempe Lake

Ross

Kentfield

Alpine Lake

Larkspu

Mt Tamalpais

Golden Gate National Recreation Area

Shoreline Highway

Bolinas Lagoon

Mill Valle

Bolinas

Mt Tamalpais State Park

Muir Woods National Monument

Stinson Beach

N

Muir Beach

0 ___ 2km
0 ___ 1 mile

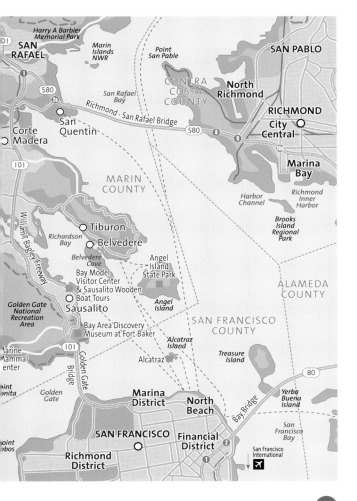

ANGEL ISLAND

SIGHTS & ATTRACTIONS
Angel Island immigration station
This designated National Historic Landmark provides a moving insight into the fate of over one million Asian immigrants to the West Coast of the United States during the early 20th century (see opposite). ❶ (415) 435-5390 Ⓦ www.angelisland.org ⏱ 08.00–sunset

Bike rentals
With no traffic, miles of trails and a stunning backdrop, Angel Island provides the perfect setting for cyclists. Bike rentals are located at the Cove Café (see page 113) and cost $10 per hour and $35 per day.

Hiking
Angel Island offers over 21 km (13 miles) of hiking trails, including two which lead to the 240 m (788 ft) summit of Mount Livermore. For those who don't fancy the ascent, the 8 km (5 mile) perimeter road leads to the island's beaches and other sights, including the immigration station and vestiges of military history.

Segway tours
A favoured means of transportation for many Bay area geeks, Segways are self-standing, self-propelled vehicles. Take the chance to hop onto one of these unique machines to tour the perimeter of Angel Island and take in some of the best views the Bay has to offer. Guided tours cost $65 per person for two hours, including

THE PLIGHT OF THE PAPER SONS

Dubbed the 'Ellis Island of the West', Angel Island was the first experience many Chinese immigrants had of the United States for much of the late 19th and early 20th centuries. Having been lured to the San Francisco Bay area by the Gold Rush, they subsequently faced discrimination, culminating in the Chinese Exclusion Act of 1882, which barred the majority of Chinese immigrants from entry to the United States. To deal with the thousands of people who nonetheless continued to arrive, the federal government began construction of an immigration station on Angel Island, which opened in 1910. Here, following their gruelling voyage across the Pacific, Chinese would-be immigrants were subjected to medical examination and intense interrogation. The stakes were high: only those from certain professions or those with a family sponsor already in the United States were admitted. The interrogation process sought to test the veracity of all claims, especially those of family ties, which were often carefully memorised fabrications by so-called 'paper sons' – migrants with only a nominal connection to their sponsor. As they awaited their fate, some arrivals carved poems and other musings into the detention centre's wooden walls, many of which are still visible today.

helmet, with a two-for-the-price-of-one deal on Tuesdays.

(415) 897-0715 www.angelisland.com Tours start 10.30 & 12.45

⬤ *Take a Segway tour around Angel Island*

Tram tours

If you prefer to sit back and relax while taking in the sights, **Angel Island TramTours** (ⓘ Information and reservations: (415) 897-0715 ⓦ www.angelisland.com) offers various tours of the park complete with an audio soundtrack explaining its points of interest. Trams leave from the Cove Café (see below) two-to-four times a day, depending on the season and level of demand.

TAKING A BREAK

Cove Café £ The only place to fill up on the island, this cute café offers sandwiches, salads, drinks and snacks during weekdays and has a barbeque oyster bar at weekends. Opening hours are limited, so make sure you stock up before setting out on a hike. ⓣ (925) 426-3058 ⓦ www.angelisland.com ⓛ 10.00–15.00 Mon–Fri, 10.00–16.00 Sat & Sun

ACCOMMODATION
Campsites

The island offers nine campsites, all of which come with running water, a food locker and a barbeque pit (campers have to bring their own tents). Reservations are required and there is a maximum of eight people per site. ⓣ (800) 444-7275 ⓦ www.reserveamerica.com

SAUSALITO

SIGHTS & ATTRACTIONS
Bay Model Visitor Center

This unique scale model of the San Francisco Bay and its

surroundings was built by the Army Corps of Engineers to recreate weather conditions, flood planning and evacuation scenarios. ⓐ 2100 Bridgeway ⓣ (415) 332 3871 ⓦ www.spn.usace.army.mil/bmvc/index.html ⓛ 09.00–16.00 Tues–Fri, 10.00–17.00 Sat

Marine Mammal Center

Five miles west of Downtown Sausalito, this conservation centre focuses on rescuing and rehabilitating hurt or incapacitated marine mammals. It is also well worth visiting the neighbouring Marine Mammal Visitor Center, which has information on the Center's work and success stories. ⓐ 1065 Fort Cronkhite ⓣ (415) 289-7355 ⓦ www.tmmc.org ⓛ 12.00–16.00 Wed & Fri; Visitor Centre: 10.00–16.00

Sausalito Wooden Boat Tours

One of the highlights of Sausalito is the houseboats and floating home communities that line its waterfront. Two three-hour walking tours hosted by local author Victoria Collela take in the historic vessels and harbours, as well as the marinas where many of the boats were – and continue to be – built. ⓐ Kiosk on the ferry landing in Downtown Sausalito ⓣ (415) 332-6608 ⓦ www.sausalitowoodenboattour.com ⓛ Sat (north tour) & Sun (south tour), departing at 12.30 ⓘ Reservation required

CULTURE
Bay Area Discovery Museum at Fort Baker

This arts and science museum is designed primarily for kids and features a number of nature-inspired exhibits including a lookout cove and a wave workshop. Nearby Fort Baker is an ex-military installation that's undergoing a major renovation by the Golden Gate National Parks Conservancy and a private developer. ⓐ 557 McReynolds Rd ⓣ (415) 339-3900 ⓦ www.baykidsmuseum.org ⓛ 09.00–16.00 Tues–Fri, 10.00–17.00 Sat & Sun. Admission charge

RETAIL THERAPY

Bacchus and Venus You don't have to go all the way up to Napa and Sonoma to taste the fruits of California wine country: with a two-floor tasting room and an art gallery looking over the Bay, this charming wine store brings the best of Northern California to you. ⓐ 769 Bridgeway ⓣ (415) 331-2001 ⓦ www.bacchusandvenus.com ⓛ 11.00–19.00

Petris Gallery In keeping with the upmarket Sausalito vibe, this boutique art shop features glassware, artwork, bronze sculptures (including an impressive collection of frogs) and vases. ⓐ 675 Bridgeway Ave ⓣ (415) 332-2225 ⓦ www.petrisgallery.com ⓛ 09.30–17.30

TAKING A BREAK

Bridgeway Bagel £ This popular brunch spot makes its own bagels and croissants and serves a good selection of hearty sandwiches and smoothies. ⓐ 3001 Bridgeway # E ⓣ (415) 332-6445 ⓛ 06.30–16.00 Mon–Fri, 07.30–14.00 Sat

Anchorage 5 ££ This diner-style breakfast and lunch spot offers a great selection of omelettes at affordable prices. ⓐ 475 Gate 5 Rd ⓣ (415) 331-8329 ⓛ 07.00–15.00

Caffe Trieste ££ Affiliated with the café of the same name in North Beach, this hospitable spot serves up sandwiches, wood-fired pizzas, pasta and amazing gelato. It also hosts live music on weekend evenings. ⓐ 1000 Bridgeway ⓣ (415) 332-7660 ⓛ 06.00–22.00

AFTER DARK
Restaurants
Thai Terrace ££ Compact, no-frills family-owned restaurant that offers great Thai food at affordable prices. ⓐ 1001 Bridgeway ⓣ (415) 331-8007 ⓛ 11.30–14.30, 17.30–21.30 Mon–Fri, 11.30–21.30 Sat & Sun

Tommy's Wok ££ Friendly Chinese restaurant that serves dishes made with fresh ingredients at reasonable prices. The mu-shu pancake-type wraps are particularly recommended. ⓐ 3001 Bridgeway ⓣ (415) 332-5818 ⓛ 11.30–21.30 Mon–Thur, 11.30–22.00 Fri & Sat, 14.00–21.30 Sun

Angelino's Restaurant £££ Stylish, family-owned Italian restaurant offering tasty pizza and pasta dishes, a decent wine selection and a great view of the Bay. ⓐ 621 Bridgeway ⓣ (415) 331-5225 ⓛ 11.30–21.30

Fish £££ As its name suggests, this waterfront restaurant specialises in fresh fish and seafood. In keeping with many places in Sausalito, its prices are steep, but the food is excellent. ⓐ 350 Harbor Dr ⓣ (415) 331-3474 ⓛ 11.30–16.30, 17.30–20.30

Sushi Ran £££ Probably the best sushi spot in the Bay Area, this upmarket restaurant has its fish flown in each day from Japan's biggest fish market. It features excellent sashimi and sushi and an impressive sake bar, but be prepared to pay for it. Reservations are strongly advised. ⓐ 107 Caledonia St ⓣ (415) 332-3620 ⓛ 11.45–02.30, 17.30–23.00 Mon–Fri, 17.30–23.00 Sat, 17.00–22.30 Sun

ACCOMMODATION

Marin Headlands Hostel £ Staying in Downtown Sausalito is not cheap, but this clean, charming hostel 8 km (5 miles) to the west of town provides dorm beds and private rooms at extremely reasonable rates. It also offers easy access to the stunning views of the Marin Headlands. ⓐ Fort Barry Building 941 ⓣ (415) 331-2777 ⓦ www.norcalhostels.org Ⓝ Muni bus: 76 from Downtown San Francisco to the Marin Headlands Visitor Center (Sun & holidays only)

Gables Inn £££ Bed and breakfast offering twelve ensuite rooms that range from bright and airy to warm and cosy. Located in a side street off Bridgeway, it is within walking distance to Sausalito's main commercial strip of shops and restaurants. ⓐ 62 Princess St ⓣ (415) 289-1100 ⓦ www.gablesinnsausalito.com

Inn Above Tide £££ Don't be fooled by the name: this is not some ancient mariner's doss house. Offering large luxurious rooms (with fireplaces), great bay views and in-room spa treatment, the Inn Above Tide is the way to do Sausalito in style. ⓐ 30 El Portal ⓣ (415) 332-9535 ⓦ www.innabovetide.com

North of the Bridge to the Valley & the Beach

Around 16 km (10 miles) north of the Golden Gate Bridge, the Muir Woods National Monument provides an idyllic escape from the hustle of Downtown San Francisco. One of the only remaining old-growth redwood forests on the Pacific coast, this natural treasure offers gorgeous hiking trails complete with a dizzying diversity of plant life and breathtaking views over the Pacific Ocean. A short distance around the coast, the small enclave of Stinson Beach offers 5.6 km (3 ½ miles) of sheltered beach perfect for swimming, surfing or sunbathing. The nearby town of Mill Valley provides a great launch pad for both destinations, with a handful of classy restaurants, shops and hotels.

GETTING THERE

It is possible to get to Muir Woods by bus from Sausalito on Saturdays and Sundays during the summer season (May to September). Take the Route 66 Shuttle from the Sausalito Ferry Terminal.

If you're driving from San Francisco, take route 101 north over the Golden Gate Bridge for around 8 km (5 miles), taking the CA-1 N (Mill Valley/Stinson Beach) exit. Follow CA-1 for 5.6 km (3 ½ miles) to the Panoramic Highway. Turn right on the Panoramic Highway and follow it until you turn left at Muir Woods road. Follow the signs for Muir Woods to the parking lot entrance.

⬤ *Walk among the giant sequoias at Muir Woods National Monument*

Countless tour operators offer one-day excursions from San Francisco to Muir Woods. A typical service is offered by **Tom's Scenic Walking Tours** (ⓣ (415) 264-6235 ⓦ muirwoodstour.com). Drop by the San Francisco Visitor Information Center at Powell Street station (see page 136) for more details.

SIGHTS & ATTRACTIONS

Muir Woods National Monument

One of Northern California's most stunning natural assets, Muir Woods offers 9.5 km (6 miles) of trails through breathtaking scenery. Hikes range from gentle to hard in their difficulty levels: the 0.5 km (⅓ mile) main loop is suitable for most bipeds, while the Bootjack Trail and the Ocean View- Redwood-Sun Trail combination provides serious hikers with more challenging propositions. A number of exhibits at the entrance to the park give visitors information on the giant redwoods and other flora and fauna in the park. ⓐ 1 Muir Woods Rd, Mill Valley ⓣ (415) 388-2596 ⓦ www.nps.gov/muwo ⓛ 08.00–sunset

Stinson Beach

Open every day year round, this stretch of sandy beach offers excellent swimming and sunbathing opportunities. While the sheltered beach is a great suntrap, the Pacific water is cold even on scorching days. During the summer months, a snack bar caters to crowds of sun seekers, while a dedicated picnic area with barbecue grills is available for those who bring their own lunch. The beach opens at 09.00 and closing times vary depending on the season. Parking can be extremely limited during the summer months as convoys of cars arrive from San Francisco. ☎ (415) 868-1922 ⓦ www.stinsonbeachonline.com

JOHN MUIR: WOODSMAN EXTRAORDINAIRE

Long before environmental activism became fashionable, Scottish immigrant John Muir decided that the natural beauty surrounding the San Francisco Bay Area was an asset worth protecting. A lifelong nature-lover and preservationist, Muir dedicated himself to the protection of the pristine wilderness areas in the Western United States, particularly the Sierra Nevada foothills and the Yosemite Valley, which he convinced congress to designate a national park in 1890. Among his many other achievements, Muir went on to found the Sierra Club, which continues to be one of the most prominent conservation organisations in the United States today. Inspired by Muir's activism, US congressman William Kent and his wife purchased a large area of old-growth redwood trees north of the Golden Gate to prevent it from being logged. Kent donated the land to the federal government, which designated it a national monument in 1908. At Kent's insistence, the site was dedicated to John Muir. Today the Muir Woods National Monument (see opposite) is one of the last old-growth coastal redwood forests in the world. Its redwood trees, some of the tallest living things on the planet, have an average age of between 600 and 800 years old.

RETAIL THERAPY

Alix and Company The perfect antidote to jewellery shopping in San Francisco's Union Square, this boutique treasure trove offers custom rings, bracelets and earrings all lovingly crafted by its long-time proprietor, Janet Alix. ➋ 55 Throckmorton Ave, Mill Valley ➊ (415) 380-0880 ➍ www.alixandcompany.com ⏰ 11.00–17.30 Tues–Sun

Claudia Chapline Gallery & Sculpture Garden Set apart from the bustle and bronzing bodies of Stinson Beach, this quaint gallery features prints, paintings, sculptures and ceramics displayed between its indoor and outdoor galleries. ➋ 3445 Shoreline Hwy ➊ (415) 868-2308 ➍ www.cchapline.com ⏰ 12.00–17.00 Sat & Sun or by appointment

🔺 *The sweeping bay of Stinson Beach*

Mill Valley Vintage Wine This long-established store carries only wines of which its owners approve. 🅐 67 Throckmorton Ave, Mill Valley 🅣 (415) 388-1626 🅦 www.vintagewines.biz 🕒 10.00–19.00 Mon–Thur, 10.00–20.00 Fri & Sat, 11.00–19.00 Sun

TAKING A BREAK

Parkside Cafe £ This casual, friendly café and eatery offers decent brunch options, including some great clam chowder, as well as scenic outdoor seating. 🅐 43 Arenal Ave, Stinson Beach 🅣 (415) 868-1272 🅦 www.parksidecafe.com 🕒 07.30–14.00 Mon–Fri, 08.00–14.00 Sat & Sun, 17.30–21.30 Thur–Mon

Surfers Grill £ Located right on Stinson Beach at the base of the main lifeguard tower, this snack shack serves up burgers, fish tacos and sodas at reasonable prices. ⓐ Stinson Beach Park, Hwy 1, Stinson Beach ⓣ (415) 868-1777 ⓦ www.surfersgrill.com ⓛ 11.00–17.00 Mon–Fri, 11.00–16.00 Sat & Sun, summer; 11.00–16.00 Sat & Sun, winter

Dipsea Cafe ££ A great place to fill up before or after a day's hiking in the woods. Serves wholesome breakfasts, including eggs and pancakes, sandwiches and boxed lunches to go, and has an extensive dinner menu. ⓐ 200 Shoreline Hwy, Mill Valley ⓣ (415) 381-0298 ⓦ www.dipseacafe.com ⓛ 07.00–15.00

The Tourist Club ££ Hidden just off the Sun and Redwood Trails in the heart of Muir Woods, this 'secret' beer house offers draught beers and traditional German munchies (pretzels, bratwursts), which hikers can enjoy on the sun deck overlooking the woods. As its name suggests, it is a private club, but non-members are welcome on the first, third and fourth weekends of each month. ⓐ 30 Ridge Ave, Mill Valley ⓣ (415) 388-9987 ⓦ www.touristclubsf.org ⓛ 13.00–18.00 Sat & Sun (first, third and fourth weekends of each month, but check in advance as private events are sometimes scheduled)

AFTER DARK

RESTAURANTS

Pelican Inn ££ Buried among the winding curves of Route 1 on the way to Stinson Beach, the Pelican offers an unlikely slice of

English pub life on the edge of the Pacific Ocean. The hospitable, wood-beamed establishment offers hearty English fare (including a Sunday carvery) and a selection of real ales. ⓐ The Pelican Inn, 10 Pacific Way, Muir Beach ⓣ (415) 383-6000 ⓦ www.pelicaninn.com ⓛ 11.30–15.00, 17.30–21.00

Sand Dollar Restaurant ££ Just a short walk from Stinson Beach, this quaint seafood restaurant offers a range of tasty dishes including barbequed oysters, fish tacos and crab cakes. Open for brunch, lunch and dinner. ⓐ 3458 Shoreline Hwy 1, Stinson Beach ⓣ (415) 868-0434 ⓛ 11.00–21.00

Stefano's Solar Powered Pizza ££ Relying entirely on solar panels for its electricity supply, this neighbourhood institution is as well known in Mill Valley for its fundraising as for its food. Its delicious array of thin-crust pizzas are all made with fresh, local ingredients. ⓐ 11 E Blithedale Ave, Mill Valley ⓣ (415) 383-9666 ⓦ www.stefanossolarpizza.com ⓛ 11.00–22.30

La Ginestra £££ A favourite of local Mill Valley residents, this family-owned Italian restaurant serves up thin crust pizza, pastas (including great homemade raviolis), and a good selection of Italian wine. (The adjoining wine bar is a good place to try out a glass before ordering a bottle with dinner.) ⓐ 127 Throckmorton Ave, Mill Valley ⓣ (415) 388-0224 ⓛ 16.00–22.00 Tues–Sat, 15.00–21.30 Sun

El Paseo £££ Classy, ivy-clad restaurant in downtown Mill Valley that offers great Japanese-inspired fine dining in exquisite

surroundings. Dishes are an east-west fusion of fresh California ingredients and artistic Japanese presentation. The three-course prix-fixe menu is a bargain. ⓐ 17 Throckmorton Ave, Mill Valley ⓣ (415) 388-0741 ⓛ 17.30–21.30 Wed–Sun

ACCOMMODATION

Mill Valley Inn £££ Swish boutique hotel in the heart of Mill Valley that provides walking-distance access to the town's shops and restaurants. Rates range around $200 for a basic queen room to over $300 for deluxe kings with private hot tubs. All prices include a continental breakfast. ⓐ 165 Throckmorton Ave, Mill Valley ⓣ (415) 389-6608 ⓦ www.jdvhotels.com/hotels/mill_valley_inn

Mountain Home Inn £££ About 6.5 km (4 miles) outside of Mill Valley and on the verge of the Muir Woods National Monument, this cute bed and breakfast offers stunning views of the Bay and truly relaxing surroundings. Rates include a full breakfast. ⓐ 810 Panoramic Hwy ⓣ (415) 381-9000 ⓦ www.mtnhomeinn.com

Pelican Inn £££ In keeping with the tone of the pub and restaurant, the Pelican Inn's seven bedrooms are a little slice of 16th-century England. Each room offers its own distinct character with a mixture of four-poster beds, tapestry drapes and gilt-framed oil paintings. Rates include a full English country breakfast. ⓐ The Pelican Inn, 10 Pacific Way, Muir Beach ⓣ (415) 383-6000 ⓦ www.pelicaninn.com ⓛ 11.30–15.00, 17.30–21.00

● *The practicalities of travel can be a voyage of discovery*

PRACTICAL
information

Directory

GETTING THERE

By air

International and domestic flights arrive into **San Francisco International Airport** (SFO ❶ (800) 435-9736 ⓦ www.flysfo.com). Transfer to the city is by BART (around 45 minutes), taxi (15 to 25 minutes), or door-to-door shuttle bus (time varies according to number and locations of drops). Those wishing to arrive directly into the East Bay can opt to fly into **Oakland International Airport** (OAK ❶ (510) 563-3300 ⓦ www.flyoakland.com). Unlike SFO, Oakland Airport is not directly connected to the BART transit system although there is a frequent shuttle called AirBart that will take you to the Coliseum BART station.

Many people are aware that air travel emits CO_2, which contributes to climate change. You may be interested in the possibility of lessening the environmental impact of your flight through **Climate Care** (ⓦ www.climatecare.org), which offsets your CO_2 by funding environmental projects around the world.

By rail

The nearest Amtrak station to San Francisco is across the Bay at Emeryville station (see page 50), although it is not directly connected to the BART network. See page 50 for other Amtrak stations which do offer direct connections to the city.

The bi-monthly *Thomas Cook Overseas Timetable* gives details of many rail, long-distance bus and shipping services in the US. **Thomas Cook Overseas Timetable** ❶ (UK) 01733 416477, (USA) 1 800 322 3834 ⓦ www.thomascookpublishing.com

By road

Driving from the south, Highway 101 and interstate I-280 will take you directly into Downtown; from the east, cars enter the city via the San Francisco Bay Bridge (I-80), which charges a $4 toll for all in-bound traffic; from the north, the only route into the city is the Golden Gate Bridge (Highway 101), which charges a toll of $5 for all in-bound traffic.

Greyhound coaches drop off and depart from the Transbay Terminal (see page 50) in South of Market.

By water

From Oakland, Alameda and Vallejo, daily ferry services arrive into San Francisco via the Ferry Building and the Fisherman's Wharf ferry terminal. From Sausalito and Larkspur, daily ferries arrive into the Ferry Building. For schedules and more information, contact the **Port of San Francisco** (ⓣ (415) 274-0488 ⓦ www.sfport.com).

🔺 *The come-hither beacon of the Ferry Building*

ENTRY FORMALITIES

Citizens from countries participating in the US Visa Waiver programme (Australia, Ireland, New Zealand, United Kingdom and most major Western EU nations) are permitted to enter the United States without a visa and to remain for a period of up to 90 days. Canadian citizens can enter the United States and stay for six months without a visa. South African visitors must obtain a visa, a process that often involves an interview at the US embassy. All entrants into the United States must complete a customs declarations form. Meats, livestock, poultry and their products are either prohibited or restricted from entering the US and all fruits and vegetables must be declared on entry. The usual prohibitions apply on dangerous items (guns, explosives, poisons etc) and travellers leaving or entering the US are required to report monetary instruments (meaning currency or cheques) valued at $10,000 or more.

MONEY

Unsurprisingly, US dollars are the only currency accepted in San Francisco. There are plenty of options to change foreign currency, including a number of bureaux de change in San Francisco Airport. Credit and debit cards are widely accepted, although grocery stores and bars will often impose a minimum limit (up to $10) on card purchases. Cash machines are available at most high-street banks, while many stores, bars and restaurants also have standalone automatic teller machines (ATMs), which are trustworthy, but which may charge higher withdrawal fees.

HEALTH, SAFETY & CRIME

San Francisco's drinking water is some of the best in the country. Its air is all the cleaner thanks to strict no-smoking policies, which cover all restaurants, bars, public buildings and public transport. Visitors can safely assume all restaurant food is safe to eat. San Francisco is one of the most pedestrian-friendly cities in the United States, and its drivers will slow down or stop for pedestrians even when the traffic light is in their favour. It is best not to test this theory, however, and pedestrians should cross major roads only when given the green walk signal.

San Francisco lies pretty much directly on top of a major fault line. Scientists have predicted that the city has a greater than 99 per cent chance of being hit with another major earthquake in the next 30 years. Tourists and residents alike can make themselves more prepared by acquainting themselves with basic safety procedures: if indoors during a quake, drop to the floor and take cover under a sturdy desk; if outside, move into a clear area away from buildings or shelter in a doorway if it is a solid, load-bearing structure.

Crime, including gun crime, is an unfortunate fact of life in San Francisco. The Tenderloin is the closest area of concern to the city's main tourist attractions. If venturing there, make sure you know the address of where you're going before you set out. Tourists are advised not to walk through the area south of Geary and east of Taylor at night.

There is a substantial police presence in many of the city's trouble spots, and police officers are most often to be found sitting in patrol cars on the side of the road.

One of the first things any new visitor to San Francisco will notice is the high level of homelessness in the city. Begging is commonplace and while it usually passive in nature, 'indigents', as they are known, will sometimes actively and aggressively ask for spare change. Knowing how best to deal with the homeless can be tricky for tourists: one sure way to make a positive difference is to buy a copy of *The Street Sheet*, a monthly newspaper written by and for homeless people in the city and sold on the streets by homeless people themselves. If you do buy one, ensure that it is from a licensed vendor.

OPENING HOURS

Most shops, businesses and restaurants in San Francisco are open every day, with some slight modifications for weekend opening hours. The only exceptions to this are shops and restaurants in the Financial District, most of which close down completely at the weekends. Restaurants are open until around 22.00, after which they will usually stop admitting customers and allow those inside to finish up. *Taquerias* are the exception to this, and stay open until the early hours of the morning. Pubs and bars usually stay open until 02.00, although some choose to close up early on weeknights when business is slow. Banks are open from Monday to Friday from 09.00 to 18.00, with many also opening on Saturday mornings. Most museums and galleries are closed one day of the week, usually Monday.

TOILETS

Public toilets (or bathrooms, or restrooms, as they're known locally) in Downtown San Francisco are few and far between.

A number of pay-to-enter kiosks (25 cents), complete with electronic doors are available in high-traffic pedestrian areas, although they often have a less-than-pleasant interior ambiance. Better facilities are available at the Ferry Building, in the Westfield Mall on Market Street, and in many hotel lobbies. Due to the high levels of homelessness in the city many businesses specify that toilets are for customers only, although desperate tourists will probably not be turned away.

CHILDREN

According to one survey, San Francisco has the lowest per-capita child population of any major US city, and Downtown in particular is conspicuous for its lack of pushchairs and toddlers. Children are not allowed into bars and an over-21 drinking age limit is strictly enforced. However, there are some great attractions in the city designed specifically for children. **The Exploratorium** (🄰 3601 Lyon St 🄣 (415) 397-5673 🅆 www.exploratorium.edu 🄻 10.00–17.00 Tues–Sun) in the Marina is an entertaining and educational arts and science museum with lots of hands-on exhibits and special events. Nearer to Downtown, **Zeum** (🄰 221 4th St 🄣 (415) 820-3320 🅆 www.zeum.org 🄻 13.00–17.00 Wed–Fri, 11.00–17.00 Sat & Sun) is an equally experiential technology and arts workshop, which gives kids (and adults) the chance to sculpt, act, sing, make movies and play a host of educational games.

COMMUNICATIONS

Internet

If San Francisco is anything, it is wired (and increasingly wireless). Nevertheless, internet cafés are not as prevalent as in many less-connected cities, mainly because many people have their own computer. Two centrally located internet cafés with publicly available computers are **Golden Gate Perk** (ⓐ 401 Bush St ① (415) 362-3929 ② 08.30–19.00 Mon–Fri, 11.00–17.00 Sat) and **Cafe.com** (ⓐ 120 Mason St ① (415) 433-4001 ② 07.00–22.00 Mon–Sat, 07.00–20.00 Sun). Visitors with their own laptops will find that nearly every coffee shop in town has wireless internet access (Wi-Fi), many offering it for free.

Phone
Due to the ubiquity of cell phones, public phones are less and less common but there are still some to be found in populous areas of the city. Visitors should look for banks of phone kiosks rather than phone booths. Local and domestic calls cost at least 50 cents.

TELEPHONING THE US
For dialling into San Francisco from abroad, use the US country code (001) plus the city code (415) followed by the seven-digit number.

TELEPHONING ABROAD
To dial out of the United States, enter 011 followed by the country code and number. Country codes:
Australia 61; Canada 1; France 33; Germany 49; India 91; Ireland 353; Japan 81; New Zealand 64; South Africa 27; United Kingdom 44

Post

Letters, postcards and parcels can be sent through the United States Postal Service (USPS) or through private-sector carriers such as Federal Express (FedEx) or UPS. USPS postboxes are identifiable by their blue exterior. Unlike in many European countries, stamps are not widely available at corner shops or grocery stores, and visitors may find themselves having to locate a post office to buy them. First-class postage is based on weight and shape, but, in general, international cards and letters (up to one ounce) cost 98 cents.

ELECTRICITY

The United States uses a 110-volt electricity supply which is accessed via two- or three-pronged plugs. Travellers from Europe, Australia, New Zealand and other countries with electrical appliances designed to run on higher voltages (between 220 and 240 volts) should check their devices for a switch to convert them to run on the lower voltage or a label that indicates that the device will auto convert. Otherwise, you will need to purchase a converter or transformer to 'step down' the voltage to make the appliances run. Many smaller electronic devices such as mobile phones can handle both inputs. In all cases, always read the label before plugging in.

TRAVELLERS WITH DISABILITIES

While its many hills can make it a tough proposition for disabled visitors, San Francisco's businesses generally have good facilities and all public buildings must be fully accessible by law. Public buses have the ability to accommodate wheelchairs and all Muni and BART stations have elevator access and level boarding to all trains. The main **San Francisco public library** (ⓐ 100 Larkin St ⓣ (415) 557-4400) has a dedicated library for the blind and print disabled on the second floor. For a downloadable copy of the official *San Francisco Access Guide* visit ⓦ www.onlyinsanfrancisco.com

TOURIST INFORMATION

San Francisco Convention and Visitors Bureau ⓐ 201 3rd St ⓣ (415) 974-6330 ⓦ www.onlyinsanfrancisco.com ⓛ 09.00–17.00 Mon–Fri, 09.00–15.00 Sat & Sun, May–Oct; 09.00–17.00 Mon–Fri, 09.00–15.00 Sat, Nov–Apr ⓝ BART/Muni metro to Montgomery St station

San Francisco Visitor Information Center ⓐ 900 Market St (lower level of Hallidie Plaza, Powell Street BART station) ⓣ (415) 391-2000 ⓦ www.onlyinsanfrancisco.com ⓛ 09.00–17.00 Mon–Fri, 09.00–15.00 Sat & Sun, May–Oct; 09.00–17.00 Mon–Fri, 09.00–15.00 Sat, Nov–Apr ⓝ BART/Muni metro to Powell St station

San Francisco City Guides Walking Tours (arranged through the main public library) ⓐ 100 Larkin St (main library); tour locations vary ⓣ (415) 557-4266 ⓦ www.sfcityguides.org

BACKGROUND READING

1906: A Novel by James Dalessandro. A gripping tale of pre-earthquake San Francisco that paints a vivid picture of a colourful, chaotic and crime-ridden city.
A Heartbreaking Work of Staggering Genius by Dave Eggers. Biography of a contemporary local author and community

organiser that gives a great insight into the life of the city.
On the Road by Jack Kerouac. Beat-generation classic that offers
a glimpse into the culture of San Francisco's famous literary
movement.
Tales of the City by Armistead Maupin. Series of novels depicting
San Francisco life over the past three decades in perceptive,
comedic style.

🔺 *Zeum is perfect for kids to try out audio-visual arts (see page 133)*

Emergencies

For all fire, police and medical emergencies, dial  911 free of charge.

MEDICAL SERVICES

Medical care in the United States is notoriously expensive and all visitors are strongly advised to ensure that they have travel insurance with maximum policy coverage high enough to meet major emergency medical expenses and/or repatriation costs. In the event of a condition requiring immediate attention, visitors should call 911 or seek out their nearest emergency room (ER). Recommended ER facilities in San Francisco include:

Kaiser Permanente 2425 Geary Blvd (415) 833-2000
Muni bus: 38 to Geary and Divisadero
St Mary's Medical Center 450 Stanyan St (415) 668-1000
Muni bus: 5 to Fulton and Stanyan
San Francisco General Hospital 1001 Potrero Ave # 107
(415) 206-8000 Muni bus: 9 to Potrero and 21st
UCSF Medical Center 505 Parnassus Ave (415) 476-1000
Muni metro: N line to UCSF

POLICE

Crime is an unfortunate reality of any big city and San Francisco has its fair share. While most visitors never have cause to contact the police, some do. For all emergencies, call 911. For non-emergencies, including reporting stolen goods, the San Francisco police department can be reached at (415) 553-0123. Crime can also be reported in person at any one of ten district police stations throughout the city. Call (415) 553-0123 for your nearest station or visit ⓦ www.sfgov.org/police. A good resource for visitors who want to check out recent crime activity in the vicinity of their hotel is the San Francisco Police Department's CrimeMAPS application on ⓦ www.sfgov.org/crimemaps

CONSULATES

Australian Consulate ⓐ 625 Market St, Suite 1800 (18th Floor) ⓣ (415) 536-1970 ⓦ www.usa.embassy.gov.au ⓝ BART/Muni metro to Montgomery St station

British Consulate General ⓐ 1 Sansome St # 850 ⓣ (415) 617-1300 ⓦ www.britainusa.com/sf ⓝ BART/Muni metro to Montgomery St station

Consulate General of Canada ⓐ 580 California St, 14th Floor ⓣ (415) 834 3180 ⓔ sfran@international.gc.ca ⓝ BART/Muni metro to Montgomery St station

Consulate General of India ⓐ 540 Arguello Blvd ⓣ (415) 668-0662 ⓦ www.indianembassy.org ⓝ Muni bus: 38 to Geary and Arguello

Consulate General of Ireland ⓐ 100 Pine St ⓣ (415) 392-4214 ⓦ consulateofirelandsanfrancisco.org ⓝ BART/Muni metro to Montgomery St station

Consulate General of Israel ⓐ 456 Montgomery St # 2100 ⓣ (415) 844-7500 ⓦ www.israeliconsulate.org ⓝ BART/Muni metro to Montgomery St station

New Zealand Consulate General ⓐ One Maritime Plaza, Suite 700 ⓣ (415) 399-1255 ⓦ www.nzembassy.com ⓝ BART/Muni metro to Embarcadero Station

Singapore Consulate General ⓐ 595 Market St ⓣ (415) 543-4775 ⓦ www.mfa.gov.sg ⓝ BART/Muni metro to Montgomery St station

A

accommodation 34–7
  Angel Island &
    Sausalito 117
  North of the Bridge
    to the Valley &
    the Beach 126
air travel 46, 128
airports 46, 128
Alcatraz 58
American football 32
Angel Island 106–13
Asian Art Museum 44, 68
arts see culture

B

baseball 32
bars & clubs 30–1
  see also nightlife
Bay to Breakers 10, 14–15
beaches 14, 110, 120–26
Beat generation 17, 64, 137
boats 58, 106, 114, 129
Botanical Garden 42, 96
Buena Vista Park 84

C

Californian Academy
  of Sciences 96–9
Candlestick Park 32
cable cars 40, 42
cafés and
  coffee shops 18, 44
  Downtown 70–1
  Central Districts 85–6

The West 99–101
Angel Island &
  Sausalito 113, 115–16
North of the Bridge
  to the Valley &
  the Beach 123–4
camping 113
car hire 56
Castro District 31, 78–82
children 44, 66, 96, 114, 133
Chinatown 62
cinema 20, 78
Coit Tower 62
consulates 139
crime 131–2, 138–9
culture 8–9, 20–2
customs & duty 130
cycling 32, 106, 110

D

dance 68, 69
disabilities,
  travellers with 135–6
driving 50–6, 128–9

E

earthquake (1906) 17, 136
electricity 135
emergencies 132, 138–9
entertainment 10–13,
  14–15, 31–4
  see also nightlife
events 10–13, 14–15

F

Ferry Building 24, 64

festivals 11–15, 33, 134
Financial District 58–77
Fisherman's Wharf 25,
  65–7
food & drink 12–13, 26–9,
  30–1, 64

G

gardens & open spaces
  40, 42, 65, 92, 96, 106–17,
  118–26
gay & lesbian scene 10,
  19, 20, 78–82, 102
Golden Gate bridge 42
Golden Gate Park 14, 20,
  42, 92
Gold Rush 8, 42, 111

H

Haight Ashbury 82
health 131–2, 138
hippies 9, 78, 82, 84
history 14, 16–17, 82, 84,
  92, 111, 121
hotels see
  accommodation

I

insurance 138
internet 133–4

K

Kerouac, Jack 137

L

Land's End trail 42, 97
lifestyle 8–9, 18–19, 20–1

M

malls 24, 69
markets 13, 24–5, 43, 62, 64
microbreweries 28–29, 76
Milk, Harvey 89
Mission Dolores 82–4
Mission District 30
M.H. de Young
  Museum 20, 97–8
money 130
Muir, John 121
Muir Woods National
  Monument 120, 121
Museum of the
  African Diaspora 44, 68
music 12, 20–2, 30–1,
  75–6, 85, 89–91, 104

N

nightlife 31–4
  Downtown 75–7
  Central Districts 89–91
  The West 102–4
North Beach 64–5

O

Oktoberfest by the Bay 12
opening hours 132
opera 22, 68

P

Palace of the Legion
  of Honour 98
Paper Sons 111
passports 130
phones 134

police 138
post 135
Presidio 9, 16, 92
public holidays 13
public transport 50–5,
  128–9

R

rail stations 50
rail travel 46, 52–8, 128
restaurants 26–9
  Downtown 71–4
  Central Districts 86–7
  The West 101–2
  Sausalito 116–17
  North of the Bridge
    to the Valley &
    the Beach 124–6

S

safety 131–2
San Francisco Museum
  of Modern Art 44, 68
seasons 10
shopping 24–5
  Downtown 69–70
  Central Districts 84–5
  The West 99
  Sausalito 115
  North of the Bridge
    to the Valley &
    the Beach 122–3
spas 33
sport & activities 32–3
Stern Grove Festival 11, 22

symbols &
  abbreviations 6

T

taquerias 27, 30, 132
taxis 46
theatre 20–2, 67
time differences 46
tipping 26
toilets 132–3
tourist information 54, 136
tours 42, 110, 113, 120
trams 52–4, 113

U

Union Square 20, 30, 51, 67

V

Victorian houses 8, 16, 42

W

walking & hiking 42,
  110, 120
weather 10, 48–9
Westfield Center 24, 44,
  69–70

Y

Yerba Buena Center 44, 69

Editorial/project management: Lisa Plumridge
Copy editor: Paul Hines
Layout/DTP: Alison Rayner
Fact checker: Lara Belonogoff
Proofreaders: Scarlett O'Hara & Judy Johnson

The publishers would like to thank the following individuals and organisations for supplying their copyright photographs for this book: Rick Audet, page 103; Owen Byrne, page 15; Wendy Cutler, page 35; Dreamstime.com (Geoffrey Kuchera, page 107; Rafael Ramirez Lee, pages 21 & 119); Franco Folini, page 88; Patricia Hofmeester/BigStockPhoto.com, page 105; John Johnston, page 1; jondoeforty1, page 112; Sutha Kamal, page 90; Karin Lau/Stockxpert.com, page 73; Jamie R. Liu, page 27; Yves Remedios, page 129; SFCVB, pages 55 & 79; SFCVB (Tom Bross, pages 45, 127 & 137; Phillip H Coblentz, pages 8–9, 43, 83 & 100; Garrett Culhane, page 11; Trish Foxwell, page 66; Jerry Lee Hayes, pages 98–9; Jack Hollingsworth, pages 25 & 33; Christine Krieg, pages 38–9; Mami Miyata, page 63; Carol Simowitz, page 7; Lewis Sommer, pages 59 & 93); Donna Sutton, page 28; SXC.hu (Kirstian Birchall, page 57; Raudel Caldera, page 41; Frank Michel, page 47; Tim Nooteboom, page 23; Sue Piozet, page 19); Miguel Vieira, pages 122–3; Luis Villa del Campo, page 77.

SFCVB = San Francisco Convention & Visitors Bureau